STAR Hiring

Contents

Chapter 1. STAR Hiring 2

Chapter 2. A STAR Recruiting Program 18

Chapter 3. Company Values 45

Chapter 4. Diversity & Inclusion 55

Chapter 5. The Hiring Strategy Kick-Off Meeting 75

Chapter 6. Sourcing STARs.. 86

Chapter 7. STAR Interviewing 128

Chapter 8. Legal Compliance 175

Chapter 9. Selection Best Practices 188

Chapter 10. Negotiating, Offering and Onboarding STARs 194

About the Author.. 224

STAR Hiring ©2018 Dan Medlin and StarHR. All Rights Reserved. Printed in the United States of America. Except as permitted under the United States copyright act of 1976, no part of this publication may be reproduced or distributed in any form or by any means, or stored in a database or retrieval system, without the prior written permission of the publisher.

Chapter 1. STAR Hiring

- ✓ The cost of a bad hire vs. the ROI of a STAR Hire

- ✓ Red flags and how to guard your company

- ✓ The secret ingredients of a STAR performer

The cost of a bad hire vs. the ROI of a STAR Hire

People make your company win!

It can cost anywhere from $5,000 to $50,000 to find and hire a new employee. To hire another new person, once you finally decide to let the first one go, you will spend 3 times your minimum cost, because your team will be extra cautious and call for more resources to fill the role again.

Loss of productivity for a bad hire can equal the full salary plus benefits and overhead of the person hired. It can include negative productivity of colleagues, a drain on the manager, even the loss of some key employees who have had enough. And a bad hire can cause you to miss deadlines, lose intellectual property, lose customers and lose sales into the millions of dollars. Reasonably, the average bad hire probably costs US companies around $210,000. That is the average cost to hire, plus 3x the cost to re-hire, plus the lost average salary + benefits of the bad hire over 1 year.

However, a great hire (a STAR) should return around 25% more than an average hire, and 250% more than a bad hire! What is this worth to you? If you know your company's current total revenue, do this simple math suggested by Lou Adler in his 2016 LinkedIn Article. Divide your company revenue by your total number of employees and multiply this by 40%. The most profitable companies on the planet return nearly $400K profit per employee. But let's say your revenue in 2017 was $1B and you had 2000 employees. That is a variable profit contribution of $200K per employee. A STAR should return 25% more than this, or $250,000. If your average salary and overhead are around $100,000, your ROI is 160%!

STAR Hiring

Know your numbers ... Do your own math...

1.	Estimated company revenue	
2.	Number of total employees	
3.	Divide 1. By 2. = Average Revenue per employee	
4.	Multiply 3. by 40% = Average Profit per employee	
5.	Multiply 4. by 25%	
6.	Add 4. and 5. = **STAR profit**	
7.	Average Salary at your company (see box at right)	
8.	Multiply 7. By 32.5% = average overhead per employee	
9.	Add 7. and 8. = average Salary + Overhead at your company	
10.	Estimated cost of your recruiting infrastructure	
11.	Total Number of hires per year	
12.	Divide 10. by 11. = Direct Cost Per Hire	
13.	Multiply 12. by 3 = Added cost to Re-Hire when one fails	
14.	Add 9. + 12. + 13. = Estimated cost of a bad hire	

Tips:

- Median salary in USA is $52K.
- Median Office Manager $76K.
- Average IT Professional $85K.

Notes:

STAR Hiring

Red Flags for Potential Bad Hires

Before I reveal the secret ingredients of a STAR hire and show you how to recognize those qualities, it is worth spending some time to analyze the signals of a potentially bad hire. You have probably seen these signs before.

Flight Risk

Typically, this candidate is motivated by highly material gains in seeking an offer from you. He or she may be compromising on cultural match issues to take your offer, whether it offers a significant gain, or just a step up the career ladder. This candidate may also desire a growth trajectory or success opportunity your organization will not be able to provide in the near term but speaks of these desires throughout your engagement. Fly away from Flight Risks.

Job Hoppers

Similar to Flight Risks, but even easier to spot, these candidates have spent no more than 18 months in any one job, over the past 3 or more employment engagements, with no plausible explanation. We can certainly understand folks who have been negatively impacted by a lay-off or two. We also can accept those who might have taken a "survival job" during tough times. But Job Hoppers have a clear pattern of no pattern. They hop between industries, roles, technologies or locations. They hop for money, but don't like the new boss. They hop for title, but don't blend with the culture. Hop out of the way of Hoppers.

Culture Mismatch

Sometimes you know immediately when a candidate comes in for an interview, and he or she is not a match to your company culture. The candidate meets you - and the team - and things just don't "click." Other times, you discover the mismatch through a good personality interview. Perhaps your culture is laissez faire, and the candidate thrives within structure. Perhaps your company requires a lot of face-time, but the candidate prefers to connect virtually. The candidate may be very attracted to your company brand, the career opportunity and the potential salary increase, so he or she will claim to be "OK" with these differences. You may be very attracted to the candidate's skills, past success, or connections in the industry. But a culture mismatch will always result in a talent loss over time. It may take just a few months, or it may take 2 years, but this person will leave you; and the skills, successes and industry contacts will leave you too. Miss the culture mismatches.

High Maintenance Candidates

I learned a few years in to my recruiting career that high maintenance candidates become high maintenance employees. A high maintenance candidate requires significant hand-holding when applying for your open position, makes more  than a few changes to the interview schedule and requires special accommodations – and not because he is disabled, but because he does not want to be inconvenienced. This candidate asks questions which he could find answers to on his own, or which have really already been answered. Perhaps these behaviors are a result of hesitance, perhaps because of ego. Or perhaps the candidate is just a little "weird." These behaviors will continue into this person's employment with you, because they are embedded within this person's personality. But here's the thing: Sometimes you need to accept the risk and move forward with this candidate. When a person can offer an immediate and sustained improvement to your profits, leadership or intellectual property, the investment into his or her maintenance is a good one. Otherwise, maintain distance from high maintenance candidates.

STAR Hiring

Unmet Expectations

Hiring managers have a laundry list full of requirements for the "perfect" candidate. Candidates also have a list of expectations about working for you. They may have heard good and bad things about the hours, the stress, the fun, or the pay at your company. During the interview process, they may not ask about these issues, 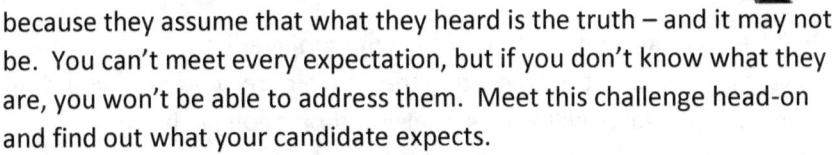 because they assume that what they heard is the truth – and it may not be. You can't meet every expectation, but if you don't know what they are, you won't be able to address them. Meet this challenge head-on and find out what your candidate expects.

Unclear Duties or Goals

While the high maintenance candidate will hound you for every last detail of their job description, day-to-day responsibilities, accountabilities and 30 – 60 - 90-day goals; the low maintenance candidate will skim past these issues to win the job. Whether it is you or your team which has been unclear, or if time just did not allow, the  candidate who joins your organization with unclear duties or goals is facing a minefield; and has a higher risk of abandoning his post within 2 years – long before your investment in training and guidance have paid off in results. Give high clarity to low maintenance candidates.

Guard your Company

Each of the "Red Flags" can be guarded early and often through a well-defined and mature recruiting and on-boarding process. Here are some practices I try to implement within my teams:

Be True in your Brand

Integrate your authentic culture into your employer branding and job marketing. It is tempting to portray the image of the company you want to be, but candidates will see the real you soon enough. If there are clear differences in what you claim to be, and what you really are in person, your investment in marketing, recruiting, travel and time will be wasted. Candidates who do not see through the ruse will become your grumblers and whiners within a year. On the other hand, make sure you do get an accurate image out online and in the public's eye, using photos, video, audio and eye-catching graphics. Use testimonials of current employees, from the "bottom" to the "top." Use the most current events. Show your engagement in the community, as well as in-house. Show your employees in all of the various work-settings possible in your firm.

Refine your Job Descriptions

Push for, drive the refinement of, and check and re-check the job descriptions for which you are recruiting. It is essential that you know who has been successful and who has been unsuccessful in the past in this role, and what qualities these people had. You must the essentials on job requirements. Which skills are "must haves" and which are "like to haves?" And after the job has been opened and a few potential candidates screened, check again on these expectations and assumptions.

STAR Hiring

Screen more Thoroughly

Integrate a more thorough pre-screening process in your recruiting architecture, which includes data gathering on the front end, and detailed conversations at each point of contact. My teams will always utilize pre-screening questionnaires on our online applications. Does this make the process lengthy? Yes. But the cumbersome application will help job hoppers de-select, and provides critical data (years of experience, technical skills and compensation requirements) to help your team select the best talent to pursue for next steps. And while you, the hiring manager may be actively involved in pre-screening calls, your recruiters need to personally connect with candidates to validate this data and explore hidden issues (visa requirements, "real" compensation needs, relocation issues, culture/personality match).

Don't Fear the Compensation Conversation

Have compensation conversations at the beginning, middle AND end of the recruitment process. If you have a full-time recruiter or headhunter working for you, this should be a firm expectation. Clarify and refine your numbers at each stage. Acquire precise information on the candidate's required or expected compensation and benefits. In some States in the USA, and in some European countries, it has become illegal to ask someone for their current compensation, but that does not mean a candidate cannot volunteer to share this information. Simply train your staff to ask for the candidate's expectations and whatever else they would like to share. See later in this workbook, in the Offer Negotiations section, more details on how each of these conversations should sound.

STAR Hiring

Stand Firm. Be selective.

A selective hiring process will include objective assessments of culture, values, skills and knowledge. Utilize scoring and chart out your results. Your assessments are working when it is quite easy to identify your number 1, 2 and 3 candidates.

Reach for the STARs

Aggressively seek top talent matches and equally push for their consideration by your hiring managers. Once you have clearly identified the core make-up of your "perfect" candidate, the "war for talent" climate calls for aggressive means to recruit and hire that person. Perhaps the perfect candidate is already in your pipeline. Get her warm, get her screened and get her in for an interview. Don't let your team ease off the gas pedal. Use all the negotiating tricks in your bag.

Over Communicate

Over-communicate with candidates during the recruiting and interviewing process. Simple and quick emails throughout the recruiting process to advise candidates of their status and next steps will really go a long way to setting expectations correctly. As a best practice, you will want to obtain an applicant tracking software that automates many of these messages. Spend time building the template messages you need, with all of the variations for different situations. As you find yourself or your team re-creating the same type of message from scratch, it's time to add it as a template in your automated emails. It is also a best practice to have these messages sent or tracked from your ATS, so that you can quickly compare who has received what message, report on your status, or even prove in a dispute that you did communicate fairly and clearly with a person.

STAR Hiring

Onboard Like a STAR

At the end of this book you will find a very detailed overview of an "Epic" onboarding process. Here is a quick preview:

Develop and follow an on-boarding communications plan from the day a written offer is sent, to the day the person starts orientation. Remember that no new hire is locked-in until they are punched-in on your clock on their first day. You still need to convince them that they have made the best decision and that they are planning for and visualizing themselves in their new role at your company.

Develop a customizable 30-60-90-day plan to outline the goals and objectives for each new hire during the on-boarding phase and throughout orientation. Provide career mapping with your new hire to allow him a chance to chart his course of growth and development in your organization. Provide quarterly follow-up and check-ins with your new hires through the first year. Gather data on team fit, manager relationship, clarity of goals, key successes and overall job satisfaction.

Discussion Questions

1. Recall a "bad hire" you have made in your past. Looking back now, were there "red flags" you might have recognized? Which ones? How long did it take before you let that person go?

2. What was the impact of that "bad hire" (revenue lost, relationships lost or hurt, lost intellectual property, lost time on a project or product delivery)?

STAR Hiring

What is a STAR Hire?

What are the unique attributes that make the difference between an average hire, and a STAR hire?

The Person

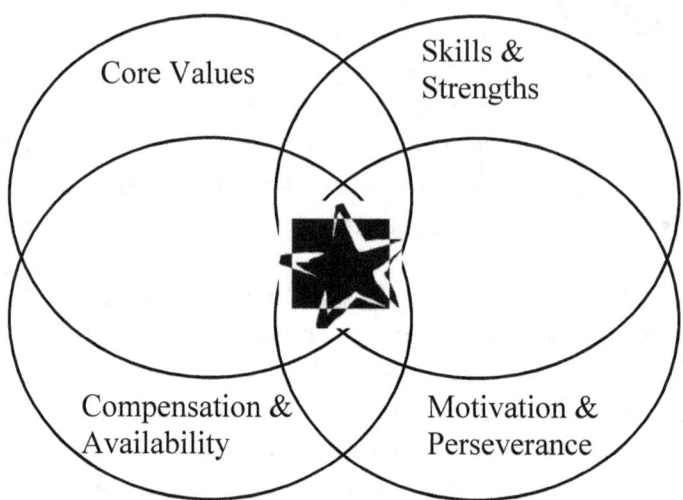

The secret to a STAR hire, vs. any other hire you will make, is trial-tested motivation and perseverance. We will discuss this more very soon, and we will discuss specifically how to assess for these traits. But first, the total package of the person you are looking to hire is the overlap of the following:
1. The candidate's alignment to your company's core values
2. The candidate's fulfillment of the skills and strengths necessary to be successful in the role
3. The candidate's proper motivation, work ethic and perseverance, and
4. An alignment of the candidate's availability and compensation requirements, to your needs and budget.

STAR Hiring

The Effort

In a STAR hiring effort, you and the candidate are **strategically aligned**. You have clearly identified your company culture requirements, the skills and experience needed, and you have advertised appropriately to attract candidates who match this profile. Your candidates therefore, are in the right industry or skillset and ready for the move into the role you have to offer.

- **S**trategy
- **T**rial-tested Talent
- **A**vailable and Acquire-able
- **R**esults-Focused ROI

The STAR candidate has the *talent you need* and offers something extra that other candidates do not – a special skill, a certain discipline, and *trial-tested perseverance*. And you have the skills and methodology (and talent) to uncover this extra ingredient.

The STAR hire is *available and acquire-able*, meaning that they will engage with you, whether they are passive or active in their search. And your recruiters and hiring managers are trained and skilled in the right search and attraction methods to engage, inform, attract and vet, these candidates.

And lastly, the STAR hire is *results-focused* and offers a clear *return on investment*. Those unique extras they offer will clearly return a profit, cut cost, improve productivity, or build the morale your company needs. Your recruiting program not only helps to uncover this potential but feeds in appropriately to your onboarding and employee retention programs to continue to stimulate *STAR performance*.

STAR Performers

There are three commonalities in STAR performers.

1. **Confidence in Skill:** STARs have the education, knowledge, training and skills to be absolutely **GREAT** at the job you need them to do. **They know this** and believe it deeply. They have explored their strengths and can communicate why they are good at what they do. STARS are *not ego-centric* or selfish about their talent, however. Their "greatness" is couched with humility, and they are <u>comfortable sharing their weaknesses and past failures</u>, because they have learned from these events and improved their core strengths as a result.

2. **Can-Do Attitude:** STARs have a "can-do" attitude. They like challenges and puzzles. Everyone gets frustrated a little, when lots of variables come at them, when priorities change or are unclear, or when answers seem just out of reach. STARS know they CAN figure out a way to push through the fog and get results. A STAR may get flustered, at least at first, but most people who observe them in stressful situations will say that they are "calm, cool and collected."

3. **Passion for Craft:** STARs have *passion* for their chosen profession and their craft. They chose their career path after considering other options and have stuck with it once they knew it was their gift. They would do it for free if they could. STARs get a strong feeling of intrinsic reward from completing their work and see the long-term benefits in what they do. If you ask a STAR what they will do when they retire, they might say they don't intend to retire, or only have something in mind for much later in life, because they just want to get better and better and do more and more of what they do best.

How STARs Achieve

1. As already said, STARs believe in themselves and are confident with their skills. Again, this is not an egotistical thing. It is based on experience of both success, and lessons learned through failure.

2. Everyone faces obstacles in life, but STARs will persevere and will overcome those obstacles. There are 2 consistent laws of achievement: There are ALWAYS obstacles, and, only those who find a way to overcome the obstacles get to their goal. STARs will be able to share examples of how they have done this in their professional life.

3. STARs succeed through pulling resources together, recruiting talent to support them and solving the puzzles in front of them. A STAR will be able to talk about the times they were faced with limited resources and confusing scenarios but pushed through and found solutions anyway.

The "T" is for Trials

The common thread throughout this analysis is that STARs **persevere through trials**. As I teach in the STAR Career Workbook, a STAR story includes the **s**ituation they are in, the specific **t**rial they faced, the **a**ction they took to push through the trial, and the **r**esults they achieved.

STAR Hiring

Just as a great novel or movie has a crisis, a great success story has a trial. Characters with depth and stories with heart involve trials and tribulation.

In my Christian faith, I am taught to consider it joy when I face trials. Trials produce testing, testing produces endurance, endurance produces strength and wisdom. When I a walk through the valley, I am developing character, so that when I am on the mountain-top, I can help others through their trials.

You undoubtedly got where you are by using your resources to overcome trials. Think of your own career and those moments when you had to persevere through trials. Are these some of your proudest achievements? You may have made mistakes and had some failures along the way. Your path may have twisted and turned to get you where you are. But through each of these trials, you learned valuable lessons, developed critical skills and gained significant confidence in yourself.

I know from many years in recruiting, that what you really want to know from a candidate is how they overcome adversity. You know that your company has significant challenges in front of it. Why else would you be hiring? All the glossy pictures of your offices and the smiling faces of your people, and all the "favorite place to work" awards you can win, won't shield your new hire of the problems they will face. Maybe you don't have the best systems or technology, or maybe you have some cumbersome policies and procedures. And even if you don't, your customers probably do!

You will see later in this workbook, a discussion of master interview techniques, and how to deal with difficult candidate behavior. One of these situations is when a candidate seems to say they have always had

STAR Hiring

success, and that results have come easy for them. You don't want this any more than I do.

You want someone who has faced trials, had some rough patches, and pushed through to become a better person. You know that <u>success which has been tested, is talent that can be trusted</u>.

A STAR candidate can identify these trials in their past and describe how they succeeded in the face of these barriers. You can use the STAR story guide to insure you are hearing the full story from a candidate, just like I teach them to tell it to you. Later in this workbook, you will learn how to do this.

Discussion Questions

1. Recall your own career and those moments when you had to persevere through trials. Jot down a short name for 2 of these. Are these some of your proudest achievements?

2. You have likely made some mistakes and had some failures along the way in your own growth. Recall 2 of these now and jot down a short name for each. Out to the right, identify valuable lessons or critical skills you gained from these experiences.

3. Recall a STAR hire you have made in your past. Looking back now, what were the qualities of that person that really set them apart from other top candidates?

4. What were the results this STAR hire brought to your team and company?

5. Where is this STAR now? What job are they in, what level and role?

Chapter 2. A STAR Recruiting Program

- STAR Recruiter DNA
- Good to Great Recruiting Program
- Building Confidence
- STAR Consultant
- Master Negotiator
- Headhunter Skills

The STAR Recruiter DNA

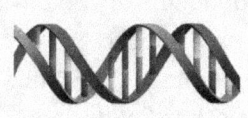

I began studying the DNA that makes up a great recruiter around 2009. I tested this hypothesis by interviewing some of the most successful recruiters I could meet, in all industries, and then by hiring recruiters to my team who had none, or very little prior experience, but who did have this 'raw talent' or DNA. This theory has proved itself time and again, and I offer it here for you, the company executive, the hiring manager or the HR Director.

STAR recruiters are gifted and talented. These qualities are natural – they are traits. They can be practiced and perfected, but a STAR recruiter is compelled to utilize them and fulfilled when they do. Most hiring managers don't have this unique combination of DNA – that's why you need STAR recruiters!

Coach

The coaching gene compels the STAR recruiter to help others to identify their strengths, to motivate them to improve on their strengths, and to hold them accountable to those plans. STAR recruiters are also adept at helping others to identify their skill-gaps and how to address them with training or practice. They will tactfully point out areas for improvement and strategically motivate others to seek an upgrade. A coach is born to encourage others when they are discouraged or when they are about to undertake new or difficult tasks. This is the person you want in your corner when fighting your biggest battle. And lastly, STAR recruiters help their candidates and their clients with insight and visibility around goals, values, culture, networking, key relationships and measurements of success.

Mediator

A Mediator is one who serves others as an intermediary or a neutral party to resolve a conflict. While you might not consider a recruitment effort to be a conflict, there are many natural tensions involved. The search for talent comes with challenges and candidates come with needs and concerns. A STAR recruiter navigates these objectively and tactfully. A STAR recruiter is also able to manage confidentiality on both sides of the negotiation, convincing both sides to share critical information that will lead to a positive outcome. Ultimately, the STAR recruiter is able to help two parties learn about the others' needs and come to a mutual agreement, assisting both sides to find a "win-win" solution.

Match-Maker

Being a great match-maker begins with developing a thorough understanding of the needs of both candidate and client. A STAR recruiter is able to translate technical or esoteric terminology into common language, which can be communicated to the public and directly to potential candidates. They also have the sales-funnel ability to gather potential candidates broadly, then filter them out to identify the specific, best matching talent for their current needs, while pipelining good, but not spot-on talent from their funnel into other matching opportunities. As a great match-maker, the STAR recruiters is skilled at the introduction, knowing that you only get one "first impression." And lastly, STAR recruiters are adept at communication on both the candidate and the client side – keeping both fully engaged and confident with the process.

Curious

A STAR recruiter is genuinely interested in the business of their clients, and the candidates they might recruit… how do they do what they do? What makes them successful? This often appears as a 'Sherlock-Holmes' type of investigation, picking up clues, finding keys and boiling it down to its 'elementary' foundations. A STAR recruiter will ask these type of questions (a lot): How do these things work? Why do them at all? Who benefits from this?

Problem-Solver

When a client, candidate, team member, friend or family member has a problem, the problem-solver gene shifts STAR recruiters into 'solution-mode.' This is not gender-exclusive – it is born from a drive to help, care and serve others. This is not an 'ego-thing.' In fact, it is often truly selfless – again – it is really a compulsion. The STAR recruiter realizes they might not walk away with a reward for their help – not every time. The satisfaction of their service is intrinsic.

Puzzle-Builder

When things get crazy and complex, a STAR recruiter will lean in to put the pieces together. They are not afraid of a mess. They take it one step at a time to solve each problem. STAR recruiters are not necessarily the most organized or conventional. They will not solve the same problem the same way every time, nor will they re-build the puzzle the same way. They know that approaching a problem from new angles brings new insights.

Salesperson

Once associated with a company, product, service, team, city, place or person, a STAR recruiter will sell the value and benefits of that thing or the amazing qualities of that person – they just cannot stop themselves! They are adept at communicating the value proposition with words and energy that inspire. Importantly, STAR recruiters are attracted to roles where they can advocate for change, progress and improvement.

Marketer

STAR recruiters are adept at assembling a message that captivates a target audience, no matter how large or small, old or new. They have excellent spoken and written communication. They are skilled with literary techniques including alliteration, hyperbole, metaphors, similes and personification.

STAR Hiring

Competitor
STAR recruiters love a good game of skill, but not of chance. They want some measure of control over their fate. Leave a group of them on their own and they will start their own internal competition. They are not afraid to lose, because they are inspired to learn, improve, and win the next time!

Process-Driver
While not always the most organized person in the room, STAR recruiters want, and will find ways to keep the process moving forward. You can count on this person to be thinking ahead, planning, and asking if you have planned.

Sense of Urgency
A STAR recruiter knows that the market demands near-immediate attention. They work on the edge of their seat, ready to get out of the meeting and take action. This is a talent and a risk. Train your STAR recruiters (like I have to discipline myself) to stop, ask 3 more questions, and then to start on their next task or project.

Discussion Questions

1. What other characteristics would you identify as prevalent in great recruiters you have known?

2. How do you personally align to the STAR Recruiter DNA? Which areas are clear strengths for you and which are not?

3. How do the hiring managers in your organization align to the STAR Recruiter DNA?

STAR Hiring

Good to Great Recruiting Program

Key elements to a successful recruiting program

<u>Process Ownership</u>

Your recruiting program, your policies and your executive team need to allow the experienced recruiters you hire to own the hiring process from end-to-end. This includes details such as when and how to advertise a role, the correct sourcing strategy to fill your pipeline, how to organize interview details, how to manage the selection process, and especially the delivery of your offers. While you may set up various support staff to assist with some of these procedures, ultimately, the recruiter who manages the requisition, should own each process.

<u>Project Management</u>

Your recruiters should be trained in project management best practices. Their DNA may not set them up as the most detail-oriented people, but they can and should keep organized using smart tools and methods. Every unique recruiting requisition is a project. This idea should be communicated and reinforced in your business. This should set the right tone for how clients engage and work with your recruiters. Hopefully it will engender some respect!

<u>Stakeholder Management</u>

A great recruiter is adept at connecting all of the resource people in the recruitment and hiring process, from hiring manager, to interviewer, to recruiting operations support, to Finance and Compensation staff, to HR systems and HR Business partners. Set up processes and workflows which facilitate the full utilization of all these resources and train them how to hand things off orderly and thoroughly.

<u>Delivery</u>

If your company is serious about growing, and about hiring STAR talent, you will have to get focused on results. In the upcoming section on a STAR recruiting program's *mechanics,* I will highlight some of the key metrics you should track and some of the measurements I recommend that you seek. Obtain technology and set up a program that facilitates accurate and timely reporting and train each recruiter how to monitor their own results. Their competitive-nature will support this.

At the same time, you must balance workloads, prioritize critical hiring needs and facilitate activity that maximizes impact. In the first of these, see my section coming up on STAR Recruiting Program mechanics. For the last of these, consider what is most important for your program in any given season... is it volume hiring, candidate experience, hiring manager satisfaction, offer acceptance, quality-of-hire, or critical skills acquisition? Encourage and allow your team to spend more energy and resources on activities that support these priorities. Postpone projects that will diminish delivery against these priorities.

Proactive Integrity

STAR recruiters anticipate problems and provide solutions before they are asked for them. Does your program facilitate this? Do your executives encourage listening to these ideas?

At the same time, STAR recruiters also must be totally honest, acknowledging issues and errors as soon as they occur, and immediately collaborating toward solutions.

Becoming a Talent Acquisition Business Partner

Our HR colleagues have professionalized the Business Partner role. Our friends in Finance and IT are now seeing the benefit of this function. It is time that Talent Acquisition adopted this as well. My position is that a STAR recruiting team might be 100% staffed with TA Business Partners or may have key leaders in the group to serve in this capacity, depending on the size and complexity of your organization. My expectation would be that TA Business Partners are senior recruiters, carrying a full requisition load, but also engaged in leadership meetings, client meetings and strategy sessions. Either way, it is good to know what this role should look like.

STAR Hiring

A Business Partner has an improved **business understanding** – the people, products, and processes that make their groups tick. They have learned the **technical** terms, critical projects, and processes that are relevant to their clients.

A Business Partner can identify **gaps in Talent** and can propose and implement changes to cover those risks. A Business Partner helps to drive their clients toward Operational Excellence and performance improvement through critical thinking, tactful questioning and resourcing their clients with tools and processes to exceed their goals.

Becoming a Talent Consultant

Whether each recruiter on your team is a TA Business Partner, or if you have identified key leaders to assume this role, a STAR recruiting program will have <u>all</u> its team members trained as Talent Consultants. What does this look like?

- They have shared **expectations** on Roles & Responsibilities with their hiring managers, interviewers, administrative support, etc.
- They are able to provide guidance to their Hiring Managers on the Hiring **process**, potential pitfalls and flexible solutions in case they run into trials.
- They are able to provide guidance on effective and **legal** job descriptions, advertising, screening techniques, interviewing practices, negotiation tactics and selecting strategies.
- They have the ability to craft the **branding** message and execute a professional marketing strategy of each role and opportunity
- They will support their Hiring Managers and interviewing teams on effective **networking**, social media, and referral gathering strategies
- They have and share their knowledge of the Talent Community and your **pipeline** of past and present candidates
- They have the ability to advise Hiring Managers on *necessary changes* to target skills, job levels and compensation ranges to most effectively fill their roles.

STAR Hiring

- They have knowledge of the **compensation** needs of qualified candidates, the approved ranges for each job at the company, and the ability to build a win-win deal for the candidate <u>and</u> the company.

STAR Recruiter Confidence

STAR recruiters are confident in their ability to advise their clients on the RIGHT hires for their organization!

- An expert on your corporate values, they know how to assess a candidate against these standards.
- They are fully involved in the screening, interviewing and selection process.
- You have trained them to be an expert on how to conduct STAR interviews, how to make proper evaluations, using rating and/or ranking; and you have equipped them to make effective hiring recommendations.
- STAR recruiters have confidence in their ability to recommend a Hire or No Hire and the are the "voice of reason" on decision-making. They know when to push-back and when to escalate

STAR Recruiters' Daily Counsel

I give the STAR recruiters on my teams the following daily counsel.

- No News is not Good News

If the hiring manager does not know that you worked on his job today, then your work is not done today. Send a quick report!

- Don't Fear the Comp!

STAR Hiring

The compensation conversation begins with the first candidate call and continues until the offer is accepted. STAR recruiters cannot afford to be afraid of these conversations.

- Be the Brand - Sell the Brand

STAR recruiters take on the colors and culture of their client organization quickly and completely. They are social media mavens and never embarrassed to shake a pom-pom.

- Know your Business

As previously stated, STAR recruiters get to know all about the technology, people, processes and future of their company. It helps them sell the brand!

- Address Red Flags Early

Know the red flags. Communicate them to your hiring managers. They are not deal-breakers, but you must proceed with candidates using all sides of the data.

- Screen Fast – Match Faster

Eliminate un-matching candidates fast and bring in matching candidates just as fast

- Always Be Closing

Stealing this phrase from our sales-friends, we use the negotiation tactics you will read about soon, early and often through the recruitment process… techniques such as "see yourself in the chair," "the clarify" or "getting yes's"

- Time kills good deals

Another phrase from our sales-friends, we know that STAR candidates will not be on the market long, and we know that they will get other offers. The longer we take to frame an offer and the longer we give a

STAR Hiring

STAR candidate to ponder that offer, the higher the risk of losing our STAR to another company.

STAR Recruiting Program Mechanics

The mechanics of a great recruiting program are equally important if you are leading the effort to build or re-shape your program.

1. **Requisition Load**

    Best Practice on requisition load is around 15 open requisitions per recruiter. If many of the roles are duplicates (the same skillset, in the same location), this can be increased to around 30. The minimum number of open requisitions to justify a full-time recruiter is around 7.

    For each recruiter managing senior management or executive roles, these figures should be divided in half.

2. **Hires per Recruiter**

    You should expect each recruiter you hire to fill about 5 to 10 open positions per month, depending on the complexity, professional and technical skill requirements. Jobs in STEM or High Tech are typically more complex and will be filled at the lower rate. Jobs in blue collar or service industries may be filled at triple this rate, if you have administrative / operations support for your recruiter (see below).

3. **Time to Fill**

    Different industries have different times to fill. STEM and High-Tech jobs take around 60 days to fill, on average, with best practice at around 45 days and trouble brewing at 90+ days. Blue collar and service industry jobs should take from 7 to 14 days to fill, with trouble brewing at 30+ days. Add 2 to 4 weeks for onboarding to calculate your Time-to-Start. Add 4 more weeks for the proportion of talent you expect to hire who will need work visas.

4. **Operations / Administration Support**
   You should plan to hire about 1 operations or administrative support person for every 3 to 5 recruiters, depending on the level of service you need, the pace of hiring you are expecting or the number of duties you are planning to assign to these professionals. Recruiting Operations can be a good starting-point for future recruiters, but it can also be a career path of its own. The personalities and affinities will differ from a person attracted to this work, to someone born to be a recruiter. Generally, your Recruiting Operations person will handle requisition approval process, interview scheduling, offer letter creation, pre-boarding and on-boarding.

5. **Sourcing Support**
   As you grow your recruiting operation, you may consider adding professionals to your team who focus on sourcing. This is the art and science of the hunt... researching, searching, finding prospects and inviting them to consider your open roles. Sourcing can also be done (as a best practice) to "pipeline" talent for future roles or hiring plans. Sourcing is a GREAT starting-point for future recruiters. The number of sourcers you need is dependent on the complexity of the roles you are filling or the scarcity of available talent. Generally, it works out to be about the same ratio as that for operations support.

6. **Recruiting teams**
   Another consideration is dividing your recruiting teams into manageable groups. This may be done regionally if you have recruiters in various locations, but I typically recommend organizing your teams by function (i.e. Engineering, Operations, Commercial) and Business Units within those functions. Admin and sourcing support should then be aligned under each team.

Essentials Tools for STAR Recruiter Success

Technology

- World-Class ATS: See "good ATS solutions" below
- All Social Media: See details in Sourcing for STARS
- Best Job Boards: See details in Sourcing for STARS
- World-class Careers Website: Your own website must be premium – if hosting through another service, make sure your page is full-branded and the host is invisible.
- Reliable Email and Instant-Messaging with Integrated Calendaring: Communications are critical. Make sure yours work!
- Video Conference technology for virtual meetings as needed

Good ATS Solutions

This book is not meant to be a sales brochure for recruiting technology. I have spent many of my years evaluating for my employers what makes up a good ATS, and this quick list are the brands/systems I would look at first when I am going to make my next purchase.

- Taleo
- Kenexa
- Lever
- Greenhouse
- SuccessFactors
- iCIMS

Your STAR Recruiting Program Business Process

I offer below, a sample recruiting business process model. You will want to design your own using Visio or PowerPoint or a similar software, and you will need to tweak it regularly, probably quarterly. Your BPM will be used to communicate to your leadership that you have a strategy, to your clients that you have a process, and to your team to keep them on-

STAR Hiring

track. Your BPM could be displayed online where it can be linked to the forms and tools it references and the persons accountable for each stage or step. Another best practice is to label each step or stage with time expected or allowed (i.e. HM review resumes submitted – 3 days).

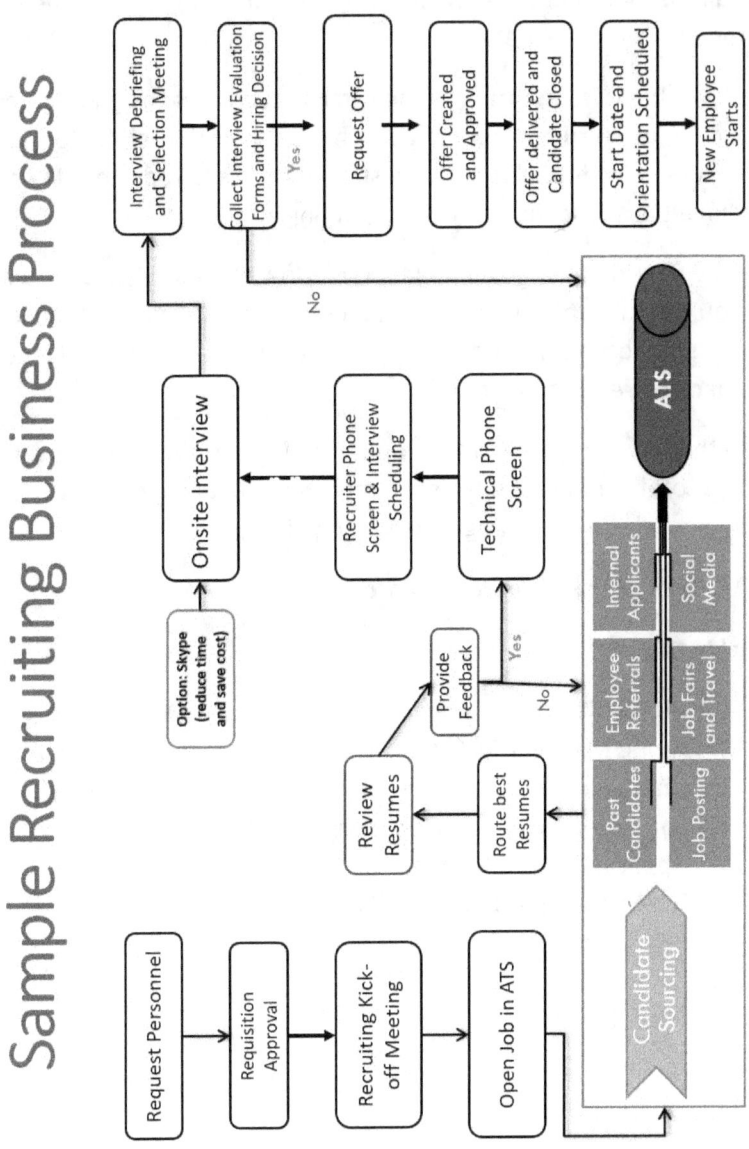

Sample Recruiting Business Process

Recruiting by the Numbers

I have spent my fair share of time on the agency side, in both small start-up and large international staffing agencies. I was resistant at first to the robotic, mechanical feeling of daily and weekly goals, because I was almost a decade into my recruiting career, but the discipline I learned was immeasurable.

I believe that it is important for any strong recruiting program to insist on individual recruiter productivity. This is especially helpful for new recruiters or for folks like me who started on the corporate side and did not have this discipline from the beginning.

Use the Recruiter Productivity Tracker below and modify it as you see fit. You can take this same format and set it up in Microsoft Excel or a similar spreadsheet program, then track your results against the goals you decide are right for your team.

Note that my tracker provides a field for both the average number as well as total number of events for each item. Keeping track of your averages helps to encourage you when your activity might taper off.

STAR Recruiter Productivity Tracker

Weekly Goals:

1. Hiring Manager Contacts: 10
2. Hiring Manager Meetings: 5
3. Unique new candidates sourced: 50
4. Sourced candidates converted to applicant: 5
5. Applicant Phone Screens: 10
6. Hiring Manager Candidate Submissions: 3
7. Interviews: 1
8. Offers: .5
9. Acceptances .25

STAR Hiring

Hiring Manager Contacts	Hiring Manager Meetings	Unique new candidates sourced	Sourced candidates converted to applicant	Applicant Phone Screens	Hiring Manager Candidate Submissions	Interviews
10	5	50	5	10	3	1

RESULTS Week Of:

Average
Total

33

Headhunter Skills

Sourcing for talent is more than just posting a job and advertising the role. STAR recruiters should be engaging in an outbound search for talent, courting them to your company and to your open roles.

This was affectionately called "Headhunting" when I became a recruiter and I'm not afraid to use the title to this day.

STAR recruiters attract experienced candidates through outbound marketing via popular social media sites, discussion boards, networking at conferences and trade shows, "cold-calling" through company directories and lastly, through some job boards.

STAR recruiters are targeted in their searches and in their contacts. You have probably received SPAM emails from many recruiters who have the completely wrong impression about your skills and experience. These are NOT STAR Recruiters. Train your team to be focused and avoid mass-spam campaigns.

Sourcing Passive Candidates

If you expect your STAR recruiters to source STAR candidates, you will need to invest in the best social media and sourcing tools to target, attract and invite candidates to consider your open roles.

Remember that the odds of getting responses from "passive" candidates are low, so prepare to load the funnel with as many potential matches as you can.

Your target candidates for experienced hiring come straight from your competition. Headhunters are not afraid to go after them!

STAR Hiring

Boolean Ninja Skills

STAR recruiters are **Boolean Ninjas!**

A Quick Tutorial

Boolean Strings are search terms run across search engines to find specific "hits" for the keywords in your search. Boolean searches can be run across Google, and in popular social media sites, like LinkedIn. Boolean searches should also be enabled in your applicant tracking system, if you have a good one, so that you can search your existing database of applicants for candidates who have already expressed interest in your company.

Basic Operators
- Use AND, OR, NOT, and ( ) to combine search terms.
- Ex: Sales AND engineer finds only candidates who have both terms. Sales OR engineer finds candidates who have either. (Sales AND Engineer) NOT Manager finds candidates that contain both "Sales" and "Engineer" but not "Manager".
- To find an exact phrase, surround your search phrase with double quotes (""). Ex: "senior manager"

Wildcards
- Wildcards are characters that can replace letters to expand a search.
- Use asterisk (*) for unknown word endings. Ex: cert* finds certify, certification, certificate, etc.
- Use question mark (?) for an unknown letter. Ex: Thomps?n finds Thompson, Thompsen, Thompsan, etc.
- Use tilde (~) to find similar spellings. Ex: roam~ finds roam, roams, room, road, roads, etc.

Site
- A site: search is also known as an x-ray search. You can search through a specific site for candidates with your desired skill set or any additional details that are a top priority for you.
- Example: site:linkedin Austin AND ".Net" AND (developer OR engineer)

Intitle or Inurl:
- Most people name their resume files using the word 'resume.' So, if you want to search Google for candidates' resumes, it's best to look for pages that include this word in their title or URL
- Example: (intitle: resume OR cv OR vitae) Austin AND ".Net" AND (developer OR engineer)

Filetype:
- Google offers you the chance to search the web for files, which is useful if you want to get access to online resumes or portfolios.
- Example: (filetype:pdf OR doc OR docx OR txt) Austin AND ".Net" AND (developer OR engineer)

The minus sign (-)
- You will need to exclude some results to get what you're looking for. It's usually helpful to get rid of 'jobs', 'templates' and 'examples' when you're looking for candidate's resumes.
- Example: "web designer" -jobs -templates -examples

Zip codes
- It's best to localize your search, if you're only looking for candidates from a specific area. For example, if your target zip code is '78701' in Austin, TX, find all zip codes in a 20-mile radius. Then, add the zip code range (from low to high) to your Boolean search to narrow down your results. It's important to include the area as well, so that Google understands your numbers are zip codes.
- Example: (intitle:resume) "web designer" 78701...78759 (TX OR Texas)

STAR Consulting Behaviors

Following are techniques I have used successfully in my own recruiting career and I teach these to my recruiters. Some of these I learned from reading and research, others from great mentors I have known. The following is a free-formed explosion of my best practices. Great negotiation skills begin with great consulting behaviors. These include:

Active Listening
The practice of paying close attention to a speaker and asking questions to ensure full comprehension. It looks like this:
- ✓ Facing forward, open-arms
- ✓ Nod and give verbal cues
- ✓ Fill in words when they are stuck

Mirroring and Matching
People feel most comfortable around those who are like them. Mirroring and matching is a technique to develop trust and rapport at the unconscious level.

- ✓ Mirroring refers to the simultaneous 'copying' of the behavior of another person, as if reflecting their movements back to them. When done with respect and discretion, mirroring creates a positive feeling and responsiveness in you and others.
- ✓ Matching, on the other hand, can have a built-in 'time lag'. For example, if a seated client uncrosses his legs and leans slightly inward while speaking, you should wait for a few seconds and then discretely adopt the same posture.

What else can you mirror and match?
- ✓ Speech Rate
- ✓ Volume
- ✓ Tone and Pitch
- ✓ Keywords and Phrases

Absorbing

The practice of accepting and soaking in the energy of the conversation. In Absorbing, you are accepting accountability for your part of the situation being discussed. It sounds like this.

- ✓ "You are right."
- ✓ "I own responsibility for that."
- ✓ "I'm sorry about that."

Reflecting

The practice of paraphrasing and restating both the feelings and words of the speaker. While mirroring is the act of repeating exactly what the other person said, paraphrasing is putting it in your own words. Adding the emotional content is the tough part. It sounds like this:

- ✓ "What I am hearing you say is…"
- ✓ "It sounds like this is a frustrating experience."

Deflecting

The practice of changing the direction of a conversation by interposing a new and equally captivating topic. This can quickly diffuse a volatile situation. It sounds like this:

- ✓ "I wonder if we could change topics for a minute, to work together on …"
- ✓ "I hear what you are saying, but let me ask you this…"

Keep Asking Questions!

Control and power in a negotiation is with the person asking the questions, and not with the person answering. Even when you think you know the answer, frame it as a question. When you feel inclined to give a speech about your great wisdom, stop yourself and ask 3 more questions. And remember that little is gained without asking for it.

STAR Hiring

Pay Attention!
It's tempting to believe that you fully understand what your client needs. You might move on quickly to respond or move forward with too little information – after all, you also want to have a bias for action, right? Take some time to tune in and ask more questions. Listen, actively. Repeat and rephrase. Get clarification and confirmation that you understand fully.

Give Value – Get Details
Sometimes, candidates are a bit reticent to share key information you may need to represent them confidently to the business. I know how challenging it can be sometimes to open a conversation early about salary, relocation, visa needs, etc. But we all know how critical it is for you to have a full picture of these variables before advancing a candidate. So here is something I have learned over the years:

If you give value to a person, they will feel indebted to you and share valuable, and often personal information back to you.

The 'giving' must be up front. What does that look like? It can begin with a thorough overview of the value proposition for the role you would like to consider them for: why should they want to join this team, take on this challenge or do this work? What do they stand to gain?

The next step may be a good analysis of their career progression, to show them how they have engineered their pathway to perfectly prepare them for this role, and what if anything is missing in their resume or CV that could be highlighted better, before sending it to the hiring manager.

And another step may be some assistance you can provide for tuning up their resume or CV, preparing for the interviews with this team, or navigating your corporate culture.

This kind of candidate care will not only get you great ratings on feedback surveys but also help to open the dialogue to many previously sensitive topics you need to uncover.

Master Negotiator Skills

As it will be discussed again in the Offering section, your recruiter should be trained and equipped as a Master Negotiator. Some of the key techniques to be mastered include:

The Give

Like the previous discussion, when you offer to give value to someone, up front, they are more likely to work with you on negotiating terms. In offer negotiations, 'The Give' might sound like this in the early stages, "Let me send you the benefits brochure and information about our Stock Purchase Plan. I want you to see the total value of the offer we are pulling together for you."

Later, as you are beginning to make a proposed offer, 'The Give' comes with some real financial value – value that you are approved and ready to give as part of the deal. It might sound like this, in a situation where you know you are going to offer a job at a level in your company that offers a 15% target bonus, you could lead with: "Let me put this on the table, because I am really excited that I got this piece for you. We want to give you a solid bonus plan in this role of 15% of your annual salary."

Clarify

Much like 'Reflecting,' When you clarify in offer negotiations, you are identifying the terms around which you can pre-close a candidate. You simply ask, "Let me see if I have this right. You are looking for a base salary of X to Y and an annual bonus target of something around X%. Is that right?"

Getting Yes's

Part of good negotiating (and selling) is getting candidates in the mode of saying yes. Asking clarifying questions is a good way to start this. Asking questions that any STAR should say yes to, is another. For example, you might ask, "Would you like to work on a challenging project where you will have impact in the company, be surrounded by caring and fun people, have smart leaders you can go to for help, but work autonomously in your day-to-day?"

The Take-Away
The Take-Away may be used in several circumstances when you have a candidate who is holding out on emotional buy-in, playing the field for other offers, or overly critiquing the opportunity you are presenting. It is a risky move, because the candidate may take the bait and leave, rather than get hooked. It sounds like this: "I'm not sure you want, or that you are ready for this role. Maybe we ought to stop the process and part ways…"

The Challenge
The Challenge may be combined with the Take-Away or stand on its own. This technique is attractive to STARs especially, because they are aware of their talents and strengths and believe in themselves. They respond well to adversity and have learned to overcome trials. It sounds like this: "Not everyone in this field is ready for this challenge. This assignment won't be easy, but it could make someone's career if they are successful. Are you up for it?"

The 'Tom Sawyer'
If you have not read Tom Sawyer as a kid, the reference may be lost on you. But essentially, in one part of the book, the hero of the story convinces other kids to help him paint a fence for free because he shows how much passion he has for the work. This technique is best used by someone who is in the same job field as the STAR you are trying to hire. So, it is great for the hiring manager to use. A recruiter can use it too, with some modifications. It sounds something like this: "You know, I get to wake up every day, come in here and bust my booty, put in crazy hours, call on crazy customers and build the most amazing product I have ever seen. I get to be a part of history! I want you to be a part of that too. How does that sound?"

STAR Hiring

See Yourself in the Chair
This technique is especially useful during the onsite interview, when you can quite literally, have the candidate go sit in the chair where he might work. In this instance, you will want to walk them around the facility, see the break room, cafeteria, fitness room, conference room, and work area. Show the candidate where morning meetings happen. Introduce the candidate to as many people as you can.

Then, through the course of phone calls, interviews and follow-ups, the hiring manager and the recruiter want to help the candidate think about and ask them if they have visualized what it will be like to work on that team, in that office, doing those projects, at your company.

Your new life ... here
When you have a candidate who will need to move to your area, either through a paid relocation or on their own, to start working for you, the hiring manager and recruiter can help the candidate think about, and ask them if they have made specific plans for moving, finding a residence, plugging into the community, helping their spouse find a job, identifying schools for their kids, etc.

Floating Numbers / Holding Back
STAR recruiters may begin to float numbers early in a candidate relationship if they sense that the person they are recruiting has a propensity for negotiating, and/or if they are not sharing any numbers of their own. Floating numbers may consist of suggesting a range or a target salary figure that is close to, but not quite at the average or target salary in the range for the role. Often, recruiters will suggest a figure that is $5K or $10K less than the target salary or average in the range, or even much lower, to "test" the candidate who says things like, "Money is not important to me," or "I'm negotiable." As the candidate will likely give a negative vibe to the "low ball" number, the recruiter can "inch it up" until arriving at the true desired range of the candidate.

STAR Hiring

Giving a Range / Holding Back
It is standard practice to give a range to uncover the desired compensation of a candidate, but one typically states a range that begins at the bottom of the range for the role one intends to offer and ends at about $5K or $10K under the middle, average or target salary in the range. Again, this "holding back" in the early stages of recruiting allows you to "increase" your offer to satisfy the candidate who impresses you during interviews. As we've said, STAR candidates will require a good, if not a great offer. At the end of the day, you may need to be making offers to STAR candidates at around 110% of the middle, average or target salary in your approved compensation range.

Pre-Closing
Pre-closing conversations begin with getting 'yes's' and continue through floating numbers and giving ranges. Pre-closing questions sound like this:

"So, if I can get you a base salary and bonus within 5 or 10% of the target we've discussed, will we have you onboard?"

"If I can get you the base salary and bonus figure we've discussed, what will you still be looking for before you are ready to accept our offer?"

Closing
Closing questions are much more direct. You are directly asking for their final "yes." One cannot be shy about this. However, you can set up the conversation for a happy ending. As illustrated before, you can lead in with the 'Gives' you are prepared to make and highlight the pieces of your offer that go beyond their expectations (and note that for a STAR candidate, there should be at least one or two pieces of the offer that exceed their expectations).

So, it may sound like this:

"I'm so glad we've made it down the homestretch for you. I felt good about your candidacy and see you doing great things in this role. Now, let me highlight some pieces of our offer that go a little beyond your previous expectations... And here are the other core pieces of our offer... So, given that we've got a great offer for a great job on a great team, can I get a firm "yes" from you? _____ Excellent! Let's start looking at your start date, and next steps for onboarding.

Negotiation Exercise

Take some time now to practice any one of these techniques. Rehearse the lines. Put your own spin on it, and work with a partner to run through the technique.

1. Which technique did you choose to try?

2. What unique spin did you put on it, if any?

3. Did it feel artificial or authentic?

4. When can you see really needing to use this technique?

5. When would you NOT want to use this technique?

Chapter 3. Company Values

To effectively hire people who fit your company's values, culture and team, you must first <u>understand</u> your company values, and how you demonstrate them.

Then you want to develop a strategy to effectively communicate those values, in job descriptions, through marketing efforts, during phone interviews and during onsite interviews with candidates.

STAR Hiring

Understanding your Company Values

This work-out will help you clarify your company's core values and their meaning. If you are hiring for your company, you must be an advocate for your company. And to cheer for your company, you must be clear on what it stands for.

List separately your company's core values, along with their meaning or interpretation, with your top 3 (as appropriate) in the number 1 through 3 slots, and the rest in no particular order.

Note: "meaning or interpretation" of a value should include "positive indicators" for each value. This means the behaviors one should demonstrate and the choices one should make, if they hold this value. You will use these "positive indicators" later in the Company Values Interview Assessment exercise, and when rating candidates and making your hiring choices.

	Your Corporate Values	Meaning or Interpretation
1		
2		
3		
4		
5		
6		
7		
8		
9		
10		

In Search of Excellence

In Thomas J. Peters and Robert H. Waterman Jr.'s 1982 work, In Search of Excellence, they found that the best-run American Companies use eight core values to stay on top. How do your corporate values compare?

1. A bias for action: preference for doing something- anything- rather than sending a question through cycles and cycles of analyses and committee reports.
2. Staying close to the customer- learning his preference and catering to them. Seeking a Win-Win solution rather than pushing the customer to take my solutions.
3. Autonomy and entrepreneurship- breaking the corporation (or my team, my job, my plans) into small companies (parts) and encouraging them to think independently and competitively.
4. Productivity through people- creating in all employees the awareness that their best efforts are essential and that they will share in the rewards of the company's success.
5. Hands-on, value driven- insisting that executives (I) keep in touch with the firm's essential values, beliefs, systems and business.
6. Stick to the best knitting- remaining with the business (core strengths) the company (I) know(s) best.
7. Simple form, lean staff- few administrative layers, few people at upper levels. (Keep it simple – don't try to be a "jack of all trades.")
8. Simultaneous loose- tight properties- fostering a climate where there is a dedication to central values combined with tolerance for all employees who accept those values. (Comfortable with ambiguity, uncertainty and change).

Clarify your Corporate Values – Now!

Is your company still working to clarify its' core values? For company founders and new corporate executives who have direct influence over the stated core values of your business, it is a critical assignment. Your public, your current or future shareholders, your employees and the STARs you wish to hire, will want to know what you believe and how you intend to demonstrate your beliefs, as a company.

Most companies seem to start with the most obvious core values: Integrity, Teamwork, Excellence and Growth. I believe that most other stated values can usually be combined back into these 4 common core values. However, other core values I have seen applied at the corporate level include: Change, Community, Creativity, Freedom, Leadership, Loyalty, Meaning/Purpose, Quality, Security, Service and Wisdom. I also like the edgy values of Entrepreneurship, Accountability and Perseverance.

You might be refining your values now and wondering how you can focus in on your central, core values or how you can identify your top 3, 5 or 7 core values from among a list of many strong interests. One technique is this simple exercise:

1. Identify **every** value you think is important for your company. You should be able to identify as many as 20 or 30 important values.
2. From this list of values place 1 star next to the ten values that are most important to you. Look for redundancies and merge any that you can, where the meaning of the values overlap and they would be equally important to you.
3. Now that you have identified your top ten, place a 2nd star next to your top 5 to 7 values using the same method.
4. Now identify your top 3 to 5 values by placing a 3rd star next to these. These would be your central core values. These are the values you would bring forward into a Mission or Vision statement for your company.

Testing your Company Values

You demonstrate your company's values when you publicly affirm and act on each value, with and among your colleagues; and when on your own. To test your previously known, or recently developed company values, analyze your personal commitment <u>to each company value</u>, and the commitment of your leadership team.

List separately your top 5-10 core values, with your top 3 in the number 1 through 3 slots, and the rest in no particular order. Analyze each core value, now individually, or as a group with your leadership team, rating your answers to the statements below.

Answer each of these seven questions separately, in relation to each individual value. Give each question a rating, using a scale from 1 being "No, not at all" to 7 being "Adamantly, Yes!"

1. Do we prize or *cherish* this value? Can we ever imagine giving it up? Does it evoke an emotional response and deep affection when discussed?

2. Have we chosen this value from *alternatives*? When we look at the list of all the values we felt were important, can we say decisively that this value was a better choice?

3. Have we chosen this value after *thoughtful consideration* of the pros and cons – and consequences of owning this value? Have we considered the political ramifications? Have we considered how our customers might react to this core value? Have we considered the impact on future employees and candidates for employment?

4. Have we chosen this value *freely*? Did we choose this value without any influence from our competitors, customers, local or national interest groups, politicians, trends, social media or other outside influencers?

5. Do we frequently and publicly *affirm* this value? Could one find repetitive recitation of or reference to this value in press releases, advertisements, job postings, event announcements, meeting plans and agendas, product releases, employee communications and even in contracts or agreements?

6. Have we *acted* or done anything about this value within the last day, week or month? Examples might include re-designing a product brochure to more closely align to this value, scheduling an employee event or community service project to act on this value, or even just simply discussing this core value in a company meeting.

7. Have we acted with *repetition*, pattern, or consistency on this value? The examples above, and similar behaviors you might identify, would be seen regularly, not mechanically, but organically, each day, week, month or quarter.

Scoring, Analysis and Action:

The scoring on this assessment has not been validated. You are free to interpret the results as you see fit. The maximum score you might achieve for each value is 49, but this is likely rare.

A score of 35 or higher would indicate that this value is central to your business and more should be done to affirm it for your employees and constituents, and externally to the public.

A score between 21 and 34 would indicate some ambivalence over this value. You may still strongly believe in this value, indicating that this is an area where you need to challenge your company going forward. What programs, policies or events do you need to consider implementing to re-invigorate your adherence to this value?

A score between 0 and 21 would indicate that this value holds no importance for your business and should be evaluated for elimination from your stated corporate beliefs.

Communicating Your Company Values to Candidates

Communicating your company values starts with the job posting itself. State your core values in every job posting and clarify what it looks like when one demonstrates these values. This is the beginning of establishing your Talent Brand, as you will learn later in the Chapter on Sourcing STARs.

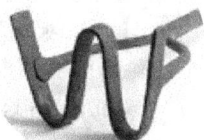

Integrate your authentic culture into your employer branding and job marketing. It is tempting to portray the image of the company you want to be, but candidates will see the real you soon enough.

Get an accurate image out online and in the public's eye, using photos, video, audio and eye-catching graphics. Use testimonials of current employees, from the "bottom" to the "top." Use the most current events. Show your engagement in the community, as well as in-house. Show your employees in all of the various work-settings possible in your firm.

During each phone screen with candidates, you should ask if they have read about your company culture, from the company website and elsewhere, and if they have reviewed your company values. You can point them back to the values statement in the job description, or to your company careers pages, where these values are discussed.

STAR Hiring

In the onsite interview phase, you can approach the assessment of a candidate against your company values in one of two different ways:

1. Assign one trained member of your interview team to complete a Values interview, in which she or he will ask behavioral interview questions centered around your core values.
2. Assign separate core values to be assessed by separate interviewers, as appropriate, within the context of their technical and professional skills evaluations.

As important as it is to assess the candidate on their ability to inculcate your company values, it is equally important that you and your interview team inculcate your company values in your discussions with candidates – role modeling for them what it looks like to be a champion of your shared values.

Having taken the assessment previously, you should know where you stand and should have ideas about what action you should take to prepare yourself for this.

Company Values Interview Assessment

You will learn in later sections about the most effective way to form interview questions and seek specific answers, and you will be given a number of sample interview questions around various key personal attributes and core values. For now, spend some time considering how you will structure an evaluation of your company values, when assessing candidates.

Following is a sample tool you can provide to your team.

Note: "positive indicator" means the behaviors one should demonstrate and the choices one should make, if they hold this value. Go back to the "understanding your company values" and check the data you wrote for "meaning or interpretation" to be clear on your "positive indicators."

Another note: I purposely do NOT use a Likert-type rating scale, which would provide for a "middle-ground" rating. I recommend that you force your evaluators toward a positive or negative evaluation. This should help to show clear differences between candidates.

Rating Guidance:

0 = no positive indications of this value
1 = meets some of the positive indicators and can develop more fully
2 = meets most of the positive indicators and "buys in" to this value
3 = meets all of the positive indicators, role model

Guidance on Hiring Recommendations:

- Candidate receives an overall average rating of less than 1.5 = 'No hire' recommendation, regardless of technical and professional skills.
- Candidate receives an average score of 1.5 – 2 = 'Hire with development requirement' if technically and professionally strong.
- Candidate receives an average score above 2 = 'Hire' if technically and professionally capable.

Company Values Interview Assessment

Rating Guidance:
0 = no positive indications of this value
1 = meets some of the positive indicators and can develop more fully
2 = meets most of the positive indicators and "buys in" to this value
3 = meets all the positive indicators, role model

Value	Interview Notes	Rate
Overall Average Rating		

Guidance on Hiring Recommendations:
- Candidate receives an overall average rating of less than 1.5 = 'No hire' recommendation, regardless of technical and professional skills.
- Candidate receives an average score of 1.5 – 2 = 'Hire with development requirement' if technically and professionally strong.
- Candidate receives an average score above 2 = 'Hire' if technically and professionally capable.

Chapter 4. Diversity & Inclusion

If your company has set a goal to increase diversity, this is not about reverse discrimination nor is it compromising on quality.

This is about <u>winning</u> with greater productivity and innovation

In this Chapter you will explore your company's goals around diversity and inclusion, your unconscious biases, techniques for recruiting a more diverse slate of candidates, and techniques for developing an inclusive and fair interview and selection process.

What is Diversity Recruiting all about?

- ➢ This is not about reverse discrimination or unfairly treating any other candidate.
- ➢ This is not about lowering the bar or compromising on the quality of the talent you hire.
- ➢ This is about <u>increasing</u> diversity at your company, thereby leading to <u>greater</u> productivity and innovation
- ➢ The market for the best minority talent is very competitive, so you must aim to get <u>more</u> than your fair share!
- ➢ This will not happen overnight – and, everyone has a role to play.

How does your company win with Diversity?

By correlating diversity in leadership with market outcomes as reported by respondents, studies show that companies with more diversity out-innovate and out-perform others. They are 45% likelier to report that their market share grew over the previous year and 70% likelier to report that the firm captured a new market.

- Harvard Business Review

Groups of diverse problem solvers can outperform groups of high-ability problem solvers, and even more importantly, from a recruiting standpoint, if groups have equal ability, functionally diverse groups outperform homogeneous groups.

- National Academy of Science

Gender diverse work teams are the most productive and profitable. Researchers estimated that transitioning from a single-gender office to an office evenly split between men and women would translate to a whopping 41% revenue gain.

- Forbes

STAR Hiring

For every 1% increase in the rates of gender and cultural diversity, there is a 3% rise in sales and a 9% rise in revenue

-American Sociological Association survey

Companies supportive of diversity report better business performance in terms of ability to innovate, (83% uplift) responsiveness to changing customer needs (31% uplift) and team collaboration (42% uplift)

-Deloitte's study on improving business performance

Diversity and Inclusion Worksheet

- Write out your company's specific diversity goal or goals:

- Are you personally proud of these goals?

- Are you committed to this goal in the face of the challenge to accomplish it?

- Have you publicly affirmed this goal?

- Have you acted to support this goal (i.e. assessed yourself, recruited talent, attended events, trained others about it)?

- What do you need to do to "Get more onboard" with your company's diversity goals?

Review of Unconscious Bias

Bias is a prejudice in favor of or against one thing, person, or group compared with another. **Unconscious biases** are social stereotypes about certain groups of people that individuals form outside their own conscious awareness.

Certain scenarios can activate unconscious attitudes and beliefs. For example, biases may be more prevalent when multi-tasking or working under time pressure.

Our fundamental way of looking at and encountering the world is driven by a "hard-wired" pattern of making unconscious decisions about others based on what feels safe, likeable, valuable, and competent. It's a survival mechanism!

We tend to organize our social worlds by categorizing and filtering. Scientists estimate that we are exposed to as many as 11 million pieces of information at any one time, but our brains can only functionally deal with about 40. We have developed a perceptual lens that filters out certain things and lets others in, depending upon interpretations, preferences and, yes, biases that we have adapted throughout our life. This tendency leads to unconscious beliefs.

Moving from Unconscious Bias to Conscious Diversity

"When we get conscious about managing diversity, we are "tuning in" to the indicators around us that tell us everyone does not see the world the way we do. While we know that intellectually, when it plays out in a difference of opinion, a different response, or a different way of being, behaving, dressing, talking -- you name it, we forget that everyone is not 'just like me.' It is at that moment that we have to wake up, realize we need to manage the diversity that is facing us and begin by thinking, "OK, who is in this mix and what are their perspectives?" -Dr. M. Elizabeth Holmes, from "Getting Conscious About Managing Diversity"

Individual strategies to address unconscious bias

- **Self-awareness:** recognize your biases using the Implicit Association Test (or other instruments)
- **Understand the nature of bias**. The strategies of categorization and filtering that give rise to unconscious bias is a normal aspect of cognition.
- Have **discussions with others** (especially those from socially dissimilar groups), sharing your biases and letting them share their own. Have these conversations in a safe space. Remain open to alternative perspectives and viewpoints.
- **Assess and change** biased language and behaviors used in hiring and management.
- Develop **concrete, objective indicators** for hiring, evaluation, and promotion to reduce standard stereotypes and implicit discrimination
- Develop and utilize **structured interviews** and develop objective evaluation criteria for hiring
- Assess and **adapt your interviewing** and management style to be more welcoming and flexible

STAR Hiring

Unconscious Bias Exercise

The first and most important step in addressing unconscious bias is self-awareness. This exercise is a VERY good start. Harvard University has developed a free assessment called the Implicit Attitudes Test. This assessment looks at your implicit associations about race, gender, sexual orientation, and other topics. Project Implicit is a non-profit organization and international collaboration between researchers who are interested in implicit social cognition - thoughts and feelings outside of conscious awareness and control. The goal of the organization is to educate the public about hidden biases. Project Implicit was founded in 1998 as a project out of University of Washington, Harvard University and University of Virginia.

1. Take the IAT. Log in at https://implicit.harvard.edu/implicit/
2. Analyze your personal results, privately. What, in your family history and experience, may have led to some of the biases that seem to be present?
3. Could any of your unconscious biases interfere with making a completely objective hire?
4. When are you most vulnerable – especially during a hiring season – because of multi-tasking, time-pressures and stress, and what can you do to diminish these vulnerabilities?
5. Gather with a group and discuss your IAT results and the most interesting things you learned about yourselves
6. Discuss your family history and both your conscious and unconscious beliefs about others
7. Share your ideas for addressing your own vulnerabilities and ask for ideas from your group
8. Discuss ideas for making your screening, interviewing and selection fair, welcoming and flexible

Review of Micro-Aggressions

We send subtle messages through our body language, word choice and behavior.

Body language is a type of non-verbal communication in which physical behavior, as opposed to words, are used to express or convey information. Such behavior includes facial expressions, body posture, gestures, eye movement, touch and the use of space.

Word choice is about using words that are very specific and descriptive. When chosen unwisely, or uncaringly, words can be sly, devious, insidious, even poisonous. These are micro-aggressions.

Microaggressions are brief verbal, behavioral, and environmental **indignities**, whether intentional or unintentional, that communicate **hostile**, **derogatory**, or **negative** biases.

Your Strategy:

1. Listen for and stop the micro-aggressions on your team
2. Insure they do not appear in your interviews.

THINK ABOUT IT NOW...

1. Do you see micro-aggressions in your team meetings?
2. Do you see micro-aggressions in social settings with your team (lunch, happy hours, hallway conversations)?
3. Do you send your own micro-aggressions out?
4. Are these subtle messages directed at one group or one person in particular?

THE CONVERSATION WILL NOT BE EASY...

1. State the facts…. "this is what I am seeing…"
2. Be clear that it needs to change… "this is not helping us and we have to change."
3. Establish a culture of respect

Examples of Racial Microaggressions

Alien in Own Land	Assuming different races are foreign-born
	"You speak good English."
Ascription of Intelligence	Assigning intelligence to someone based on their race
	"You are so articulate."
Color Blindness	Statements indicating that a person does not want to acknowledge race
	"When I see you, I don't see color"
Criminality / Assumed Criminal Status	Assuming a person is dangerous or criminal based on race
	A woman clutches her purse when a person of color walks past.
Denial of Individual Racisim	Denying racial bias- perhaps after being confronted with your own.
	I'm not racist, I have black friends."
Myth of Meritocracy	Stating that race does not affect life success
	"Everyone can succeed if they work hard enough."
Patholologizing Cultural Styles	The notion that the dominant cultures are ideal.
	"Why don't you celebrate Christmas?"
Second-Class Citizen	Assuming a person of a different race is lower class
	Mistaking a person of color for a service worker
Environmental Microaggressions	Microagggressions that occur on a larger scale
	TV shows featuring particular races over others

Diversity in your attraction strategy

We must address our language and approach toward candidates which limit diverse applicants.

More inclusive Job Descriptions

The first thing to consider is that job seekers may be already wondering, "Does this company value diversity?" If you want more diverse job candidates, say so! It's the quickest and easiest way to get the word out. Let all candidates know, through your advertisement that you value different cultures, genders, races, etc.

Check your very long list of requirements

As a recruiter for many years, I have seen job descriptions morph over time, from bureaucratic to stripped-down and meaningless; from a "kitchen-sink" list of requirements, to no expectations at all. None of these strategies helped candidates, nor did they increase inclusivity.

All candidates, including those from minority groups, want to know:

- What is going on in your company that necessitates this role?
- What is exciting about this specific role and how does it impact your mission?
- What will I do in this role, especially the more challenging duties?
- What will my goals be and how will we know when I reach them?
- What education, years of experience (roughly) and career background must I have to have a chance to interview for this role?

But for some of the candidates you want to attract – women and/or minorities in particular - there are a few areas of caution.

A long list of nice-to-haves will actually **deter** female and some minority candidates from applying. Studies have shown that men apply for jobs when they meet only 60 percent of the outlined qualifications, but women don't feel confident to apply unless they meet 100 percent. If you feel compelled to list your preferred qualifications, make sure they are differentiated from your requirements, and splice the language with these kinds of descriptors:

- "familiarity with…"
- "working knowledge of…"
- "comfortable with…"

In what ways do you need to reduce and trim down your job requirements?

_____
_____
_____
_____

Check for gender-biased language.

A study reference in Forbes showed that gender diverse work teams are the most productive and profitable. Researchers estimated that transitioning from a single-gender office to an office evenly split between men and women would translate to a whopping 41% revenue gain.

A study published in the *Journal of Personality and Social Psychology* revealed that women refrain from applying to jobs with descriptions that use masculine words. Sounds almost obvious. They might think, "Why set myself up for discrimination?" Or, it could be the thought that "I don't want to work for a company which is so overtly masculine." Either way, you will not diversify if you don't attract women to your opportunity in the first place.

Overt examples of gender-biased language might include the use of "he" and "his" when describing the job or your requirements, or terms such as "man hours" or "manpower" in the job description. Then you might consider whether you are using metaphors which are appealing more toward males, vs. females, such as "touchdown" or "tackle" instead of "win" or "take on."

Textio is a free tool that analyzes and improves job descriptions for effective language and format. Based on data from third-party job boards and company data, Textio can tell which words and phrases are more likely to attract male or female applicants. Similarly, Gender Decoder for Job Ads highlights gendered wording and identifies if a job ad is masculine- or feminine-coded.

What Do Job Descriptions Really Say?

Job descriptions play a critical role in recruiting female talent and often provide the first impression of organizational culture. If a company offers flexible work arrangements but instead emphasizes long hours in its ad, this may inhibit qualified candidates from applying, especially those with primary care responsibilities.

Even subtle word choices in a job description can have a strong impact on the application pool. Research has shown that masculine wording of job descriptions, including adjectives like "superior," "competitive," and "determined," results in women perceiving that they would not belong in the work environment.

In what ways do you need to gender-neutralize your job descriptions?

STAR Hiring

Gender-Biased Language Exercise

The job description below for a Mechanical Engineer at a top firm has many words that are perceived as stereotypically masculine, which could inadvertently deter women from applying. *See if you can spot all 10.*

Job Title: Mechanical Engineer

Company Description: We are a top engineering firm dominating the marketplace, boasting many leading clients. We are determined to lead the industry; our success stems from consistently challenging our competition.

Essential Functions
- Challenge the status quo by creating superior product designs through the development and testing of specifications and methods.

Knowledge and Skills
- Superior design skills
- Exceptional conceptual skills
- First-rate technical knowledge
- Strong communication skills
- Proven experience with production planning

Working Conditions
- Tight deadlines and multiple priorities, requiring decisive decision making in a fast-paced environment.
- Willing to work outside the standard 9-5 schedule, including early mornings, evenings, and weekends as required by tight project deadlines.
- Ability to work independently in a competitive work environment.

Education & Experience Requirements
- Bachelor's degree and 3-5 years of work experience

STAR Hiring

Key:

How would you re-phrase the following:

1. Dominating
2. Boasting
3. Challenging
4. Competitive
5. Superior
6. First-rate
7. Proven
8. Tight Deadlines
9. Decisive decision making
10. Outside the standard 9-5... including early mornings, evenings, and weekends

Check for age-biased language

The primary concern against using age-biased language is the screening out of older candidates. There is a legal reason not to do this in the United States, that being the Age Discrimination in Employment Act (ADEA) of 1967. ADEA protects certain applicants and employees 40 years of age and older from discrimination on the basis of age in hiring, promotion, discharge, compensation, or terms, conditions or privileges of employment. But secondly, you are missing an incredible opportunity to diversify your ranks with talent who are seasoned with a more diverse range of life and professional experiences.

Think for a while about times when you have specifically screened out older candidates. What assumptions were you making?

___*Overqualified?* What are you afraid of in hiring an overqualified candidate? If you can hire a person with more years of experience, more wisdom, more life experiences and potentially more skills, why wouldn't you get them?

___*Cannot afford them?* If you are clarifying the expected compensation range of the candidate and your budget for your role, early and often in your recruiting process, and the candidate is clear that she or he will be satisfied with your budget, this is a great deal for you company.

___**Won't stay around long?** Time and again, we see that younger workers move around more and have less longevity with their employers, vs. older employees.

___**Less productive?** The 2010 Cogito Study, proved that older workers' productivity was *more* consistent than younger workers'. These included tests of cognitive abilities, perceptual speed, episodic memory and working memory. Older workers' performance was more stable over time, they learn and remember more, and take less time to learn than younger workers.

What does Age-Biased Language look like? Age-biased language, like gender-biased language, can be overt and obvious, or subtle. Overt and obvious would be using statements like, "We are looking for a young, energetic talent to lead our team." More subtle age-biased language to change might be terms like "fresh", "bright", "energetic", or "new".

Check for racially biased language.

Racially biased language will ALWAYS detract women and minority candidates from applying to your jobs or pursuing opportunities with your company. Remember, companies with more diversity out-innovate and out-perform others. They are 45% likelier to report that their market share grew over the previous year and 70% likelier to report that the firm captured a new market.

Review again the material on microaggressions for examples of racially biased language and attitudes in your company. Avoid words, images or situations that reinforce stereotypes and that imply all people of a particular race or ethnic group are the same, are less than equal, or are undesirable.

STAR Hiring

Where do you need to address this problem in your company?

[ ]

In a job description, one might be stating goals or requirements in such a way that implement a microaggression. An overt example would be, "No Lazy people should apply for this role!" A subtle example would be, "Must have a strong work ethic and be committed to completing one's tasks." While you might think this should be acceptable, really on the face of it, you can see that this requirement is unnecessary to state. No one wants you to hire someone who is **not** committed to the task! To some candidates, you might be saying, "I believe that you are lazy, so I really don't want to interview you."

One might actually overtly discriminate in a job posting, and if you spot it, you should root it out immediately. For example, one should never require things like "White, Anglo, or non-immigrant." Subtle terms like "bright, clean or fresh could imply a racial preference or communicate a racial micro-aggression.

Another word of caution: if an employer relies exclusively on word-of-mouth recruitment and referrals within a specific ethnic group, and it results in new hires primarily from the same ethnic group, that may violate the law. This is referred to as "adverse impact."

Notes:
_____
_____
_____
_____
_____

Check your Images and Photos for your Ads

When choosing photographs or illustrations, consider the balance of women, men and people of color. Also, be conscious of the relative positions of the people in your images and their actions. Nonverbal messages conveyed by portraying some standing and others sitting, or some pointing to or working with equipment while others are passively observing, imply status differences. Such implications, whether subtle or direct, are unrealistic in the modern workplace. Work with your artists and photographers to update graphic content.

Notes:
_____
_____
_____
_____

More inclusive sourcing strategies

To begin with, if you source for talent (advertise, search and invite talent to consider your opportunity) in places that appeal to a wider group than those you traditionally employ, you'll automatically increase the diversity of candidates you consider. Generally, the main sites like LinkedIn, Indeed, Monster and CareerBuilder all attract a broad base of candidates, including minorities. You can go one step further by advertising and contacting candidates through mediums which are built specifically for minority groups. Leverage professional associations that cater to diverse candidates. Reach out to networking groups, alumni associations and other networks that already function as a hub. Consider advertising in publications and attending conferences or networking events sponsored by those organizations that cater to diverse populations.

Hopefully, some diversity already exists in your organization. Ask your team for referrals. Diverse employees are connected with diverse job candidates. Get them involved. Ask them to share your job posting on their social media, to reach out to good talent they know, and to refer good candidates for the role.

To hire diverse job candidates, a company may also need to be open to someone whose background does not fit into the usual mold. For example, consider hiring someone who comes from a different industry, or who has slightly different skills.

Notes:

More Inclusive Interview Slate

Your shortlist or interview slate is the first place to address a more inclusive interview process. If diversity is truly a priority, you will want to ensure that there are under-represented candidates in the candidate pool for all open positions, and especially when you get to the interview phase. Many companies go for the "quick hire," choosing candidates that are former colleagues and referrals from employees and friends. Although you may fill positions quickly, unless your company is already quite diverse, "quick hires" often lack diversity.

A 2016 study published in the *Harvard Business Review* found that if there are four candidates and three are female, there's a 75 percent chance a woman will be hired. The study also found that when there were at least two persons of color on the short list, they were nearly 194 times more likely to get hired. Interestingly, if the slate is two men and two women, the odds of a woman being hired are 50/50. But when there are three men and one woman, the chances of a woman being hired is statistically zero. This is likely because the one female candidate is viewed as a "token." With more than one female or person of color on

STAR Hiring

your shortlist, now they are just other candidates, which is what you want them to be.

Notes:

_____
_____
_____
_____

More Inclusive Interview Process

Design an interview based on the skills and attributes needed for success in the role, nothing more. If you identify ahead of time what it takes to be successful in the role you are filling, you should be able to interview each candidate according to those criteria – including the STAR quality of having experienced and persevered through trials.

Ask every candidate the same questions and measure each candidate the same way. You can and should interview every candidate the same way, for the same qualities. This takes planning and preparation.

Select your interview team carefully and **include a diverse slate of interviewers.** Consider whether you have a decent representation of gender and race on your interview team and do your best to balance it out, for all candidates who interview.

Avoid Interviewer Bias errors, discussed on the following slide. In later sections we will discuss interviewer bias errors and how to avoid them.

Train all interviewers! Using this training, and other great materials you can find, make sure that your interviewers are trained on behavioral interviewing skills, legal matters, and how to provide for a good candidate experience.

STAR Hiring

Include all the interviewers in the evaluation process and insist on sticking to the pre-defined evaluation criteria.

Notes:
_____
_____
_____
_____

More inclusive interview experience

It's NOT an interrogation!

I have seen managers who express a desire to confuse, disturb, frustrate or pressure candidates during interviews. Their attitude is that the workplace is tough and challenging and they need someone who can "survive" their environment. Clearly their focus is on the wrong thing. Go and "take the plank out of your own eye" before you interview like this. Improve your work environment, repair relationships and make your workplace enjoyable – then you will be able to sell your employee experience rather than having to find candidates who are willing to survive it.

Be welcoming

The little things do matter! Make sure someone is designated to greet your candidate on arrival, show them around the office, and escort them to the interview room. Have some water, coffee or other beverages available. Make sure they know where the restroom is and offer them a break before and during the interview.

Leave time to talk about your work culture, work-life balance, office amenities, benefits and more.

STAR Hiring

Designate one key interviewer to discuss the company and team culture

It is often a best practice to designate one key interviewer to be your "culture-guy." But this should not just be a social role. This person should also be tasked with evaluating the candidate against your company's core values, as we discussed in the previous section.

Every interviewer should allow time for candidate questions. During this time, be open and honest about your experience working at your company

Notes:

_____
_____
_____
_____

Final Discussion Questions Around Diversity in your Hiring Practices:

1. People feel differently about this advice. What is your opinion?

2. What research have you done to support your opinion?

3. What experience do you have with under-represented populations?

4. Is your company staffed sufficiently with under-represented populations? Why or why not?

5. If it is not, what is your personal commitment and plan to address this?

Chapter 5. The Hiring Strategy Kick-Off Meeting

A Critical First Step to launch every recruitment effort

- Shared understanding of Project
- Establish expectations and timelines
- Build a Partnership for success!

Why have a Kick-off Meeting?

The Hiring Strategy Kick-off Meeting is sometimes referred to as the "intake meeting" or "alignment meeting." This is a critical FIRST step in an effective recruitment effort.

This meeting helps you and your recruiter gain a shared understanding of the recruitment project, establish expectations and timelines and build a Partnership for success!

What typically happens if you skip this step?

Without this meeting the hiring manager and recruiter are disengaged and lack partnership. Both sides will make poor assumptions about their shared duties, and because of the lack of clarity in the search parameters, your recruitment effort will see significant lost time.

> *When should this meeting happen in your agreed-upon recruitment process?*
> – *BEFORE recruitment starts!*
> – *Establish this as policy and reap the rewards!*

It is my estimation that for every 30 minutes you dedicate to this meeting, you can shave 25% off your time to fill, if the meeting is done properly and the agreements and expectations established in the meeting are upheld through the project.

Imagine a worst-case scenario of a job taking 120 days to fill in your company. An effective 1 hour hiring strategy meeting with firm commitments can reduce that to 60 days. Let's say you've been successful reducing your time to fill to 90 days, through basic program efficiencies. Implementing this strategy can bring that down to 45 days. If you are currently seeing a time to fill of around 60 days, and you mandate a 1-hour kick-off meeting, you can start to see jobs filled in as little as 30 days.

STAR Hiring

Without a Hiring Strategy Kick-off meeting, or when the agreements and expectations established in the meeting are not upheld through the project, there is a strong possibility that you will have to start your recruitment effort all over when the project fails.

You may find yourself canceling unfilled requisitions, re-writing job descriptions and re-booting your search efforts. This is often because of mis-alignment. Set up the infrastructure now to include this critical meeting, and encourage your teams to invest ample time, and follow-up meetings, to get completely aligned.

Hiring Manager Challenges

Scheduling - "No time!"
As we've seen, the Hiring Strategy Kick-Off Meeting, it's follow-up meetings, and/or re-alignment meetings when needed, will actually save you time and increase efficiency. Invest the time up-front and reap the rewards later.

No meeting rooms
The Hiring Strategy Kick-off meeting can be held virtually, onsite, offsite and/or outside of regular hours. There are really no excuses. If your recruiters have the "Driver" DNA they should have, they will find a way to make this meeting happen.

Nothing new - we already know this
Often-times, recruiters will hear from hiring managers that the job description is the same, it is just a repeat effort, and no changes are in play; so, no alignment meeting is needed. But we have learned that something new is revealed every time we have a Kick-Off... why someone left the team, a new strategy that is being used, or a new technology that you are using. Press in to make this critical meeting happen every time you open a new requisition.

You do your job – I have my own

There is a reason why the "Hiring Manager" title is assigned. You (if you are the hiring manager) OWN the hiring of this person. This new hire will report to YOU. The recruiter, if he or she is a STAR recruiter, is fully equipped to counsel and advise, and to keep things moving, autonomously. But this is a partnership. The role will not get filled without the Hiring Manager and his or her team fully engaged and fully involved.

Recruiter Challenges

Half an hour is not long enough

STAR recruiters will often say that 30 minutes is just not enough to ask the questions they need to ask and set expectations appropriately. Yes, an hour – or more would be better. Sometimes you will get it. Often you will not. I say the first thing you need to do after that first meeting, is schedule a 2nd meeting / follow-up, weekly, or bi-weekly catch-up meeting. Make this the last thing you agree on before wrapping up and keep refining your plan each successive meeting and each engagement.

Too Many Chiefs

Another problem that STAR recruiters will point out is when there are too many decision makers. Perhaps the Hiring Manager's boss is involved, plus one or two top members of the team – and each of them have different concepts of success for the effort. I teach my recruiters to get everyone "in the room" – all decision-makers and stakeholders, let everyone state their case, and then to require identification of a top decision-maker. At the end of the day, the hiring manager needs to be given authority to call the shots –the requirements for the role, who will move forward to interviews, and who will get the offer. Otherwise, chaos will reign.

Lackluster-ness

STAR recruiters may be faced with a lack of enthusiasm for new ideas (cutting edge sourcing strategies, etc.), a lack of openness to changes to the requirements, or needs of the hiring team or a lack of openness to

STAR Hiring

different ways to fill their role (a different level of candidate or a different kind of employee, i.e. contractor or remote worker).

I counsel my recruiters to show their stakeholders the competitive intelligence...
- Where is the talent for this role?
- What does it take to reach them?
- How many contacts does it take to get a candidate?
- How quickly will the best candidates get other offers?
- What will it cost to hire them?

If the intelligence stacks up against filling the role with their current list of requirements, or without adapting to new search methodologies, then you can show them the potential for success in adopting your recommendations.

Notes:

Standard Content for the Kick-off Meeting

I offer for you here a template of a standard Hiring Strategy Kick-off Meeting. Adapt and format this to fit your needs.

1. **Role Details**

    - Job title / Internal vs. External posting (what is the most effective title to attract the best candidates?)
    - Who is the primary hiring manager? Who is back up?
    - Grade Level, Compensation, and Package Structure
    - Reason for the position opening (budgeted addition, replacement, group expansion, etc.)
    - Review of the job description & skill requirements
    - What are the "must haves" versus the "nice to haves"?
    - Top 3 essential technical AND non-technical hard skills
    - Ideal candidate attributes, experience level and key resume identifiers
    - Qualifying or pre-screening questions/criteria TAA can ask on initial call.
    - Position Travel Requirements/Percentage
    - Relocation, yes or no, international or domestic only?

2. **Value Proposition**

    - Organizational hierarchy, team size/dynamic, location geography, and reporting line structure
    - What is this group responsible for and what specific partners or clients would this person be working with?

- What new things are happening in the business that this person will touch?
- How will the person in this role contribute to the goals of this team and department?
- Why should a person want to join this team?
    - Team culture and interaction
    - Manager / Leadership style
- Potential avenues for long term career progression and/or skillset development for the candidate
- What's the biggest challenge or most interesting problem this person will solve?
- How might certain aspects of the role change over time?

3. **Ideal Candidate / Sourcing Strategy**
    - Top CORE VALUES needed in your ideal candidate (STAR)
    - Top STRENGTHS needed in your ideal candidate (STAR)
    - Most likely functional roles / job titles / role profiles that top candidates would currently hold
    - What type of professional would see this challenge as an ideal way to grow their career?
    - Target companies, company types, company size and locations for these candidates
    - LinkedIn groups, etc. that you can pull talent from
    - Referrals - leverage hiring manager's network and the team's networks.
    - Overview of the recruitment and/or sourcing strategy

STAR Hiring

- Provide hiring manager with a model of how and where you find talent normally

- Internal and External job posting; and referral submittal process (define pros/cons, recruitment strategy, and structure).

- Discuss market realities of acquiring desired talent at established job grade and budgeted salary

4. **Timelines and Expectations:**

    - Set expectations for candidate submittal, resume review, and feedback (24/48 hr. turnaround preferably).

    - Set expectations on turn-around time for Screening, Scheduling Phone Interviews, Scheduling Face-2-Face interviews (Secure Admin support for this), Selecting candidate for Hire and Approving Offers.

    - Interview process (phone and face-to-face)

        – Who will be involved in the interview/selection process?

        – Who could stand in as back up?

        – What criteria will the different interviewers measure/focus on?

    - Hiring time frame: when does the person need to be on-board?

    - Advise HM on current Talent Acquisition metrics for time to fill, any specific trouble-spots that might arise in the process and ways to move through them quickly.

    - Any travel/conferences/holidays/sabbaticals coming up with you or your team?

    - Discuss post-interview roundtable and final candidate selection meetings and expectations

Follow-up after Strategy Kick-Off

Follow-up is critical to an effective strategy kick-off. The recruiter owns this. Managers should expect it...

1. **Schedule next meeting**

    - The first agenda items are those left untouched from the first meeting

    - Then you want to begin discussing sample profiles of candidates you have sourced

    - And lastly you want to begin preparing for your interviews, as covered in the Interview Planning section to follow.

2. **Follow-up with Hiring Manager to keep him/her engaged on the recruitment effort**

    - See sample email on following page.

    - Provide tools and links to resources created by your company or found on the web so Hiring Manager can return to this email as a resource through the recruitment effort.

3. **Initiate the Marketing and Sourcing Strategy**
    - Recruiter should help hiring manager to launch a campaign to advertise and market the role
    - Recruiter and hiring manager should be on "same message," sharing content and links.
    - Hiring manager should seek referrals from employees and from professional network. Recruiter can provide templates

Notes:

SAMPLE

RECRUITER FOLLOW-UP
AFTER HIRING STRATEGY KICK OFF MEETING

Thank you for the kick-off meeting to discuss the [external title] role, requisition number [#] on your team. The job is posted and active and you are set up as hiring manager.

Here are some helpful links for you to navigate the hiring process at our company:
1. Staffing Process Overview: [link to your intranet page]
2. Talent Acquisition Toolkit (resources and templates: [link to your intranet page]
3. Branding guidelines and resources for our company: [link to your intranet page]

Here is the internal posting for our employees who want to apply to the role: [link]
Here is the external posting for candidates we find outside of our company: [link]

I have kicked off the job marketing campaign for this role by posting the following on my social media feed. Please share this with your team and invite them to "Re-Share" this post to their feeds for broad coverage of this opportunity. Here is the link: [link]

Another best practice is to send an email around to your team to seek referrals of top talent we may collectively know. I have drafted that for you below. Please CC me when you send this out.

STAR Hiring

I will be in touch with next steps and further best practices to keep this search moving – and to show you some top candidates. Please remember to continue thinking about the following:

1. Update your social media profile so that we can network together and source top candidates, and encourage your team to do the same
2. Using the critieria we have set out in the job description, what standards will determine if candidates are a match? How will you rate and rank your candidates?
3. Decide who will be on your interview team, what you want each person to focus on with candidates, and how they should evaluate candidate responses.
4. Then, prepare an email to recruit these interviewers to your team and get them ready for their focus.

Let me know of any specific tools, resources, support or guidance you may need.

Thank you,

RECRUITER SIGNATURE

Notes:

Chapter 6. Sourcing STARs

- Your Talent Brand
- Job Descriptions & Advertising
- "Real" sourcing and networking
- Screening STARs

Your Talent Brand

Your Talent Brand is how your people think and feel about working at your company and what they share socially about working at your company. It is your "reputation" in the marketplace. Your reputation is also spread by spouses and friends and even vaguely known contacts, who pick up on the message and feel inclined to communicate positively or negatively about your company. And most importantly, your Talent Brand is also communicated by candidates who engage with your company for job opportunities.

Because of the social sharing phenomenon, it is imperative that you know the Strengths, Weaknesses, Opportunities and Threats to your Talent Brand.

Talent Brand SWOT Analysis

- **Strengths: what about your company <u>is</u> attractive to candidates?**

- **Weaknesses: what about your company is <u>not</u> attractive to candidates?**

- **Opportunities: what about your industry is attractive to candidates?**

- **Threats: what about your industry is <u>not</u> attractive to candidates?**

How do you influence your Talent Brand?

Define and promote your core values – internally first

Your founders or leaders may have already spent time defining your core values, so leverage that work and promote them and integrate them into your everyday culture and performance management strategies. Then integrate your core values into your job marketing, candidate screening, and interview assessment.

Match the compensation and benefits of your peer companies

Your compensation or HR team should spend some time with a good set of salary and benefits survey data to ensure that you are on par with your peer companies.

There is no excuse for lagging your peers around compensation, benefits, social sharing or employee referral incentives, in a competitive talent market.

Engage with your employees regularly to assess their satisfaction

Remember, your brand starts with your own employees and what they say about working for your company. Find out what is bugging them and what is thrilling them, and then do more of the latter.

Encourage above and beyond performance with appropriate rewards

You may be surprised to learn that great employees actually don't want to be coddled or spoiled – they are happy with a challenge and want to be driven to grow and develop their talents.

Market your Employer Value Proposition (EVP)

Your EVP should be clearly presented with words and images, extolling your company core values, employee benefits, retention, satisfaction and engagement, community involvement and your various rewards programs. Your EVP should be most clearly represented on your company's own Careers or Jobs page on your corporate website – a page that should be professionally developed and maintained. Then every social media post and job advertisement should echo this message.

Encourage employees to share socially

Your employees will be active on social media. You cannot, nor should you try to prevent this. Equip them with plenty of stories and easy ways to share updates about the good things going on at your company. You can facilitate this with social sharing tools such as Hoot Suite, Hubspot, Buffer and Linkedin's Elevate platform.

Engage your employees in your recruitment program

If you don't already have one, or even if you do, take a look at best practices for Employee Referral Programs. Programs today will include an easy method for sharing job openings with their network, a specific method for tying the referral to the employee and an appropriate employee referral incentive – a cash award.

Here is a potential hack: while doing your survey work on salaries and benefits, see if you can get data on what companies are offering for Employee Referral bonuses. Just know that it does not need to make them rich, but it needs to be significant.

With respect to the method for sharing jobs with one's network, I advocate firmly for a referral to be "qualified." What that means to me is that the employee making the referral must

1. Know the candidate personally
2. Understand the qualifications of the candidate
3. Collect the candidate's resume
4. Upload the candidate's resume to your system and complete a few fields that indicate the candidate's qualifications
5. Link the referral to a specific role for which the employee believes the candidate is qualified

Job Descriptions and Advertising

The *beginning* of a winning talent sourcing strategy

Your job description is only the beginning of your talent sourcing strategy. Remember that you are not considering the STAR recruiting process because you think that you can post a job and just wait for great candidates to apply. We have also established that STARs are frequently "checking out" the available job market for opportunities to grow in their careers. A great job description is a must to attract both the active job seeker and the passive one that you invite to apply to your role. Here are the key components of every job Description:

Title really does matter!

The job title is the very first thing a candidate sees. It's a headline, a billboard and a vital marketing tool that goes a long way in attracting qualified candidates. When candidates are actively searching for roles, their search results will lean on the effectiveness of your job title first, then keywords in your job description second.

Therefore, with your job description, be clear, relevant to your industry, up-to-date with terminology, and specific with the core skill needed. Be honest about the seniority level. You want qualified candidates... not under nor over-qualified. Only put "senior" in front of actual senior level positions. However, don't use "junior" (no one wants a "junior" role). Only use "director" or "manager" if the position actually directs or manages.

An introduction that sizzles: See below

Employer Value Proposition: See your Talent Brand / EVP

Why should I want this job?

Ultimately every candidate wants to know that they will grow, develop and benefit from taking on a new job. Tell them how they will do this in your role! Will you provide great mentors, training, customer engagement, access to executives, cutting edge tools or processes?

STAR Hiring

Every STAR wants to know...

Take some time to answer these questions now, or use this form in your Hiring Strategy Kick-Off Meetings

- What is it like on your team?

- Who will I work with?

- Who will I learn from?

- How will I grow in this role?

- What does success look like?

- Describe your ideal candidate

How do I make it sizzle?

Lead with your Brand

You want your whole job description to sizzle, and you do this by leading with your brand.

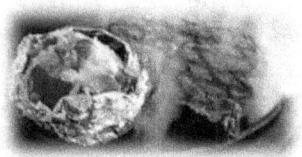

Include an introduction that highlights your company, its position in your marketplace and your potential for success.

Lead with your EVP

You also want to lead with your employer value proposition (EVP), not requirements. Many job advertisements lead with what you companies from a top candidate. You might as well say you are looking to screen OUT as many candidates as possible, as quickly as possible. If you want an ATTRACTION strategy, lead with the answer to question, "Why would I want this job?"

Use Action verbs

An action verb is a verb that expresses physical or mental action. It describes for the candidate what they need to be able to do. STARs are action-oriented and want to know clearly what is expected of them. A list of potential action verbs is included at the end of this section.

Personalization & Conversational

Using "you" and speaking to the candidate in your advertisement gives it personalization and makes it conversational. See examples of this in the Job Description sample provided in further pages.

Explain yourself

Be clear about what your product or service is, and how the work of this individual will contribute to the delivery of that product or service.

Questions with answers

An edgy way to advertise (but not new), is to ask a question, like "What will your day-to-day look like?" Then, answer it.

Be vulnerable and honest

Is this a tough job? Say so! Are things chaotic for your company right now? Admit it! This gives candidates a "Realistic Job Preview" as we will discuss later in the interviewing sections, and STARs who are looking for a good challenge or problem to solve, will be attracted to the opportunity.

Speak to your target audience

To speak to your target audience, you first need to know who they are. Are they boomers or millennials? Are they geeks or are they social animals? Are they experienced, mature leaders, or are they looking for leadership and mentoring? Do your research on the proper ways to communicate to your target audience and test the language you plan to use on people who currently fit that target.

Don't sacrifice diversity!

Address your language and approach toward candidates which limit diverse applicants. Go back and review the chapter on Diversity and Inclusion if you are still in doubt. Check for gendered, aged and racially biased language, using this book and the tools I recommend.

STAR Hiring

Job Description Action Verbs

- **Administer:** To provide or apply something; to put something into effect
- **Advise**: To give an opinion or suggestion to someone about what should be done
- **Analyze:** To study something closely and carefully
- **Approve:** To officially accept (an idea, action, plan, etc.)
- **Arrange:** To organize the details of something before it happens; to plan (something)
- **Assess:** To make a judgment about (something)
- **Assign:** To give someone a particular job or duty; to require someone to do a particular task
- **Authorize:** To give power or permission to (someone or something)
- **Collaborate:** To work with another person or group in order to achieve or do something
- **Communicate:** To give information to someone by speaking, writing, or moving
- **Conduct:** To direct or take part in the operation or management
- **Confirm:** To make (something) definite or official
- **Consolidate:** To join or combine together into one thing; to make (something, such as a position of power or control) stronger or more secure
- **Consult:** To talk about something with (someone) in order to make a decision
- **Coordinate:** Bring the different elements of (a complex activity or organization) into a relationship that will ensure efficiency or harmony
- **Counsel:** To give advice as a result of consultation
- **Create:** To produce or bring about by a course of action or behavior
- **Delegate:** To assign responsibility or authority; to appoint as one's representative
- **Deliver:** To take and hand over to or leave for another; To come through with
- **Design:** To plan and make (something) for a specific use or purpose
- **Develop:** To create (something) over a period of time
- **Direct:** To cause (someone or something) to move in a particular direction

- **Disseminate:** To disperse throughout
- **Distribute:** To divide (something) among the members of a group
- **Document:** To record (something) in written, photographic, or other form
- **Draft:** To draw the preliminary sketch, version, or plan
- **Edit:** To alter, adapt, or refine something to bring about conformity or make it better
- **Educate:** To train by formal instruction and supervised practice especially in a skill, trade, or profession
- **Estimate:** To give or form a general idea about the value, size, or cost of something
- **Evaluate:** To judge the value or condition of (someone or something) in a careful and thoughtful way
- **Examine:** To look at (something) closely and carefully in order to learn more about it
- **Facilitate:** To help (something) run more smoothly and effectively
- **Formulate:** To put into a systematized statement or expression; to prepare according to a formula
- **Gather:** To bring (things or people) together into a group; to choose and collect (things)
- **Guide:** To direct, supervise, or influence usually to a particular end
- **Implement:** To carry out, accomplish, especially to give practical effect to and ensure of actual fulfillment by concrete measures
- **Inform:** To give information to (someone)
- **Initiate:** To cause the beginning of (something); to start or begin (something)
- **Integrate:** To combine (two or more things) to form or create something; to make (something) a part of another larger thing
- **Interpret:** To explain the meaning of (something)
- **Investigate:** To observe or study by close examination and systematic inquiry
- **Maintain:** To keep in an existing state (as of repair, efficiency, or validity); to preserve from failure or decline
- **Manage:** To have control of (something); to take care of and make decisions
- **Modify:** To change some parts of (something) while not changing other parts

STAR Hiring

- **Monitor:** To watch, keep track of, or check usually for a special purpose
- **Motivate:** To give (someone) a reason for doing something
- **Negotiate:** To discuss something formally in order to make an agreement
- **Obtain:** To gain or get (something) usually by effort
- **Order:** To put in order (arrange); to give an order to (command)
- **Organize:** To arrange or form into a coherent unit or functioning whole
- **Oversee:** Supervise (a person or work), especially in an official capacity
- **Plan:** To think about and arrange the parts or details of (something) before it happens or is made
- **Prepare:** To make (someone or something) ready for some activity, purpose, use, etc.
- **Present:** To formally talk about (something you have written, studied, etc.) to a group of people
- **Process:** To subject to or handle through an established usually routine set of procedures
- **Produce:** To cause (something) to exist or happen; to cause (a particular result or effect)
- **Provide:** To make (something) available; to supply (something that is wanted or needed)
- **Recommend:** To say that (someone or something) is good and deserves to be chosen
- **Reconcile:** To find a way of making (two different ideas, facts, etc.) exist or be true at the same time
- **Recruit:** To find suitable people and get them to join a company or an organization
- **Research:** To search or investigate exhaustively
- **Scan:** To look at (something) carefully usually in order to find someone or something
- **Schedule:** To plan (something) at a certain time; to appoint, assign, or designate for a fixed time
- **Search:** To carefully look for someone or something; to try to find someone or something
- **Select:** To choose from a number or group; pick out
- **Serve:** To furnish or supply with something needed or desired

STAR Hiring

- **Solicit:** To approach with a request or plea
- **Solve:** To find a way to deal with and end (a problem)
- **Supervise:** To be in charge of (someone or something); to watch and direct (someone or something)
- **Supply:** To make (something) available to be used
- **Test:** To use a set of questions or problems to measure someone's skills, knowledge, or abilities; to apply a test as a means of analysis
- **Train:** To form by instruction, discipline, or drill; to teach so as to make fit, qualified, or proficient
- **Translate:** To change words from one language into another language; to explain (something) in a way that is easier to understand
- **Verify:** To establish the truth, accuracy, or reality of

STAR Hiring

A very good Job Description example...

Why is this a good company intro? See if you can spot the...
1. Mission
2. History
3. Success
4. Great Product
5. Personalization
6. Relevance

About Lifesize

At Lifesize, we understand the power of connecting people to make the workplace great. For more than a decade, Lifesize has been at the forefront of video collaboration, delivering high-quality solutions designed to bring people together. We combine a best-in-class, cloud-based video conferencing experience, with award-winning, easy-to-use devices that are designed for any conference room, so you can connect to anyone, anywhere. It's a meeting experience like no other. Our video conferencing solutions are designed for the demands of today's modern enterprise, yet fully accessible to businesses of any size. For more information, visit www.lifesize.com or follow the company @LifesizeHD.

Let's discuss the other key winning elements found below...
1. Title: Specify key skill in title and identify job level (senior) in title
2. Job intro: Personalized, New & Relevant, ID your product. Talk about the team – why would they want to join it?

Title: JavaScript/React Developer, Senior Software Engineer

Would you like to work on a high performing team developing advanced user interfaces with the latest technology for our next generation video communication products? Lifesize is looking for an experienced developer to join our client software development team in Austin. This team is responsible for the development of our customer facing web-

STAR Hiring

based UIs as well as our React based Mobile, Desktop, and endpoint apps.

About the role:
(good use of action verbs)
- You'll develop cutting edge web/desktop/and mobile interfaces; from concepts through requirements, use cases, implementation, unit testing, and on through live deployment.
- You'll write readable, well-tested JavaScript and TypeScript code in a team of engineers who are working to continuously improve the codebase.
- You'll work with developers, designers, and product managers in a collaborative agile environment to deliver product improvements on an ongoing basis.
- You'll solve high priority customer issues and get fixes deployed with a fast turnaround time.

Some of the perks you'll get working in Lifesize Engineering:
(Employee Value Proposition)
- Pick your preference of a Mac or PC environment, and we'll get you hooked up.
- Come to work in our convenient Barton Skyway location, which is close enough to downtown and Zilker Park to have access to the best of Austin.
- Be amazed at the programming flow time you'll establish in our non-open engineering floor plan, which includes a mix of private and shared offices.
- Take time off when you need it with our unlimited vacation policy and our flexible work schedule.
- Eat free breakfast tacos on Mondays and Wednesdays and enjoy a catered lunch on Tuesdays and Thursdays.
- Take a break in our fully stocked break rooms with all the snacks and drinks you need.
- Recharge yourself in our free onsite yoga classes and gym.

STAR Hiring

About you:
(Specify years of experience – not a range – always use a "+")
- 3+ Years Commercial/Enterprise Software Development
- 1+ Years Modern JavaScript (ES6+)
- 1+ Years React/Redux

Ideally, you will...
(STARS want to know what the "Ideal Candidate" looks like)
- Be adept at delivering working UIs from wireframes and detailed acceptance criteria.
- Understand the redux pattern including where and how to apply it.
- Be fluent in JavaScript build tools like Webpack, Babel, CSS preprocessors, and unit testing frameworks like Jest.
- Be capable of driving towards a goal independently and proactively solving problems with minimal oversight.
- Have experience in architecting single page data-driven applications and developing efficient and maintainable solutions.
- Have excellent troubleshooting skills, and a passion for fixing customer issues.
- Be adaptable enough to work between multiple projects and technologies within a condensed time frame.
- Be comfortable working with Git in a continuous integration environment.
- Offer constructive feedback during code reviews as well as positively receiving and executing on the feedback offered by others.
- Have at least a basic understanding of databases and servers with a desire to learn more.
- Have excellent communication skills with the ability to explain technical issues to non-technical co-workers.
- Have a bachelor's degree in Computer Science, related field, or equivalent real-world experience with a firm grasp of Software Engineering/Computer Science fundamentals.

STAR Hiring

<u>You'll impress us even more if</u> you have experience with some of these: ***(STARS want to know how they can "shine")***
- WebRTC
- TypeScript
- React Native
- Electron
- Native Mobile (iOS or Android)
- Native Desktop (Windows or Mac)
- AWS
- SOLID design principles

I offer this previous job description example because of the MANY very good things it does. This example offers you many ideas to create your own modifications. However, the only criticism I have for the previous job description is its length. The truth is, most candidates will not read beyond about 600 - 900 words. LinkedIn research shows that job postings under 300 words had significantly higher application rates. My professional guidance for you is to stick to the middle (300 – 600 words). You want enough words to adequately describe your company, team, job and requirements, and not too few – which may lead to a bunch of unqualified or meekly motivated job applicants dropping into your applicant pool.

Job Description Template, pretext

Every job posting from your company does <u>not</u> need to look the same!

In fact, more variety is better. However, the main 3 headings always survive: Summary, Duties and Requirements. To these, I add Core Values.

Consider doing something a little more creative with your job descriptions, using the template that follows, and various modifications.

Job Description Template

Why would I want this job?

Include a brief hook about the role and why you are recruiting for it, including opportunities within the role for growth and impact. This section should capture the interest of the candidate. Why should they want to join your team?

What will I do in this job?

- *Describe the goals, objectives, and accountabilities for the role*
- *Do not describe the person you'd like to hire or the skills they need to have*

What are you looking for in top candidates?

- A Bachelor's degree in a relevant degree program is required.
- A Master's degree is preferred. *(eliminate this if not needed)*
- A minimum of ___ years of directly related experience is necessary for consideration.
- Expertise in …
- Success at …
- Detailed knowledge of …

What are the core values I need to demonstrate?
We are proud to have a set of core values that reflect our unique culture and guide our decisions. These values are assessed during the recruitment process:

- .
- .
- .
- .
- .

Job Application Format Guidance

You will likely have a standardized application form, either separate or integrated with your job postings on your corporate careers' website. Following is a sample standardized form. In all cases, with regard to job application forms, you should follow and understand these things:

- ➢ Be Brief – Candidate drop-off is high at this stage. Don't lose great candidates because you think you need to collect massive amounts of data that you <u>can</u> collect later. Decide what is essential.

- ➢ Allow candidates to refer to their resume where possible. Provide a means to either upload or attach their resume to their application so that you can streamline this process.

- ➢ Provide clear indications of what items are required before a candidate passes over these fields and tries to save or submit their application.

- ➢ Dates should be optional on education, military years, etc., to protect candidates from potential age discrimination. You can collect this information later when you do your background checks and education verification.

- ➢ Create a system where candidates can re-use one application to apply for multiple opportunities at your company, but also allow them to attach different versions of their resume which may be tweaked to fit different roles.

Job Application Template

Our company wants to make the job application process as quick and simple as possible. Please attach a complete resume with your previous job history, education, certifications, licenses and any other relevant information to support your application, then complete the following applicant Information:

Applicant Name:					
Home Phone:					
Other Phone:					
Email Address:					
Home Address:					
City:		State:		Zip:	
How did you find us?					
Position(s) applying for:					

Are you applying for?

Temporary work	[ ] Y or [ ] N
Part-time work?	[ ] Y or [ ] N
Full-time work?	[ ] Y or [ ] N
If hired, on what date can you start working?	___ / ___ / ___
Annual Salary desired:	$_____

STAR Hiring

Personal Information:

Are you over the age of 18?	[ ] Y or [ ] N
In compliance with federal law, all persons hired will be required to verify identity and eligibility to work in the United States and to complete the required employment eligibility verification form upon hire. Please initial that you understand this requirement.	_____ Your Initials
Are you able to perform the essential functions of the job for which you are applying, with or without reasonable accommodation?	[ ] Y or [ ] N
If no, describe the functions that cannot be performed	
(Note: We will comply with the ADA and consider reasonable accommodation measures that may be necessary for eligible applicants/employees to perform essential functions.)	
Have you ever been convicted of a criminal offense (felony only)?	[ ] Y or [ ] N
If yes, please describe the crime(s), when and where convicted and disposition of the case.	
(Note: No applicant will be denied employment solely on the grounds of conviction of a criminal offense. The date of the offense, the nature of the offense, including any significant details that affect the description of the event, and the surrounding circumstances and the relevance of the offense to the position(s) applied for may be considered.)	

STAR Hiring

Job Advertising Choices

You have a few options when it comes to job advertising. Just remember that most advertising attracts "active candidates" and not "passive candidates." To reach candidates who are successfully pursuing careers in the job-field you are hiring, you will need outbound sourcing.

That said, even a passive candidate will want to see your role advertised to know that the opportunity is legitimate when you call her, and some "passive" candidates will stumble upon your advertisement and click on it out of curiosity.

The first and most important place to advertise your open role is on your own company website. This advertisement should be tied in with your applicant tracking system, so that when candidates click to "apply" for the role, their resume and contact information goes into your database where you can track their candidacy. A well-presented careers/jobs page on your company website should get a few good applicants on its own, as candidates search via Google or other search engines. Make sure your website manager knows proper search engine optimization (SEO) to insure your jobs are found.

The next thing to consider is whether you want to pay for an automated job distribution tool that allows simultaneous job posting to multiple sites. This software, integrated with your ATS, can take your job from your website and post it out to the web. You will need subscriptions on the various sites this tool will post out to, but the time saved in quickly choosing where to send the job once you have created it in your ATS, will rapidly advance your sourcing strategy. Some new ATS' on the market actually have this software built in. If not, some good services to consider include the following. Note that you do not need to be a major enterprise business any more to be able to use an ATS, and many solutions are on the market which are tailored to small and start-up businesses. Just make sure you pick a system that can grow with you!!!

Good ATS Systems (and related) out there today
- Taleo
- Kenexa
- Greenhouse
- SuccessFactors
- Lever
- iCIMS
- Zip Recruiter

Automated Job Distribution Tools and related
- Talroo
- Broadbean
- PostingPal
- JobMP
- Bullhorn Reach

Major Sites to consider for advertising your role:

Indeed.com is the most popular job posting site in the world. It started off as a job search engine that would crawl the web and index every job ever published along with offer no-cost job postings. Now Indeed has become an extremely popular job board. Indeed has a huge resume database and claims over 180 million unique visitors per month and is available in 50 countries and 28 languages.

LinkedIn is the world's most popular social network for professionals. It is fast becoming a place to post jobs and handle talent management due to its enormous reach and growth in active users. LinkedIn is mostly suited to white collar jobs as its growth has predominantly been professionals with desk jobs. It's a good place to post jobs to fill more senior roles also. With the rise of social recruiting, LinkedIn is a must. It's like a giant social resume database.

STAR Hiring

CareerBuilder is a general posting site, is one of the most trafficked job sites in the U.S. and is trusted - it has direct relationships with 92% of Fortune 500 companies. Pricing is based off or number of posts purchased. Buying job postings in bulk gets you a better price.

Dice.com focuses on information technology, engineering professionals, and high-level tech positions, and typically features more than 90,000 tech job listings. The most recent available numbers put Dice.com at having 3 million registered tech professionals, 65% with more than 10 years of experience in their field and 75% with a bachelor's degree or higher. Dice.com charges customers per post, with discounts for bulk buys.

Monster.com is a great job board for a wide range of jobs and has a great resume database. Pricing is based on the number of postings you buy - the more you buy, the cheaper each post is.

Glassdoor is best known for allowing employees to post reviews of employers and management, and to report their salaries for everyone to see. But Glassdoor is also one of the largest hiring websites. Cost starts at $99 per job post and varies based on location.

Talent Sourcing
"Yes, I'm a headhunter!"

Sourcing for talent is more than just posting a job and advertising the role. We call that the "post and pray" method. Zip Recruiter recently appropriated this term in the context of their solution to advertise your job posting on "hundreds of sites." That's still posting and praying! They've updated their technology to include emails out to prospective candidates to invite them to apply. Now they are getting closer.

If you have a full time, part time or agency recruiter working on your role, you should be expecting that professional to be engaging in a concerted outbound search for talent, and once they find good-matching talent, they should be courting them to your company and your open role(s).

We often refer to these candidates as "passive," but they may be just as active and ready to move as someone who clicks on your ad... you just need to get to them before your competitor, who is just "posting and praying" for good applicants. Whether active our passive, your goal is to attract them to your posting which they have not yet seen and convince them to consider it.

The courting of good candidates can look different for different industries and levels of candidates, but generally, it should include:

1. Advanced Searching techniques using Boolean scripts (more training on this soon) that one can save and re-use, as well as advanced searching tools provided by the platform, such as Talroo/Jobs2Careers, Indeed, LinkedIn, etc.

2. A well-crafted invitation scheme to attract targeted prospects to your opportunity. This may include multiple contacts, in which you layer in more details about the opportunity as prospects express an openness to hear more, or it may be an

"all-in" communication that directs candidates to apply online if they are interested. The higher the level of the role, or the more niche the skillset, the more I recommend the first approach.

3. Outbound calls or text messages from professional recruiters to target candidates, especially when emails or other electronic communications go unanswered or are not useful.
    a. Targeting outbound sales candidates
    b. Targeting candidates who do not sit at a desk
4. In invitation to have a call with a recruiter who can explain the employee value proposition and gather basic details about the prospect's employability.
5. An opportunity to speak to a hiring manager or delegate to ask questions about the role, the team and the technical or professional requirements.
6. A request to the prospect to officially apply to the job so that you can track their candidacy in your ATS
7. Convert the prospect to a candidate as soon as they are ready and align them to your normal screening and interviewing process, as similarly as possible to all other applicants to the role.

Sourcing Experienced Hires

Your target candidates for experienced hiring come straight from your competition! You know who these companies are because you have worked there. A successful recruiting partnership includes you tapping in to your network of former colleagues and known industry peers who would be great for your company.

Some of your target candidates may also work for companies which are customers or vendors. While your recruiters may not want to target applicants from your customers, as your industry circulates great talent, many of them will be attracted to your company.

Sourcing Passive Candidates on Social Media

If you expect your recruiters to source STAR candidates, you will need to invest in the best social media and sourcing tools to target, attract and invite candidates to consider your open roles.

You typically attract experienced candidates through outbound marketing via popular social media sites, discussion boards and lastly, through some job boards. Hiring managers and their teams MUST help with this effort! Learn how to create your own fantastic posts to promote the job you need to fill.

Through your accounts, your recruiters can spotlight and advertise key roles, run advanced searches for matching talent and set up project folders to share profiles with you and get your feedback.

While your recruiter is sourcing "passive" candidates, **this is not a passive activity on your part**.

A good search begins with clear requirements. Know what you "must have" vs. what is "nice to have." It is also helpful to have a resume of someone already successfully doing the role, or a similar one, or an "ideal candidate" so that we can "clone" that resume in our searches.

Once the search is on, your recruiter will need feedback on which candidates make a good match to your requirements. Get back to them quickly with a "thumbs-up" or "thumbs-down."

You can also advise your recruiter on the messaging that might go out to certain identified candidates... for example, if they are known by you or your team, the recruiter will want to message this to the target candidate to "warm them up" to your opportunity.

Remember that the odds of getting responses from "passive" candidates are low (think about how often you reply to unsolicited Linkedin Inmails), so prepare to load the funnel with as many potential matches as you can, and expect to only end up speaking to very few people – but those prospects should be very good matches to your requirements!

Other Social Media and Business Networking Sites

EventBrite is another tool you should consider for finding events, meetings and networking opportunities. Eventbrite is a global marketplace for live experiences that allows people to find and create events in 190 countries. Set up your own account, or just visit the site and "Browse Events" to find interesting and relevant meetings and events in your area to source and meet interesting candidates.

Meet Up (www.meetup.com): Meetup is a social networking site dedicated to making it easy for anyone to organize a local group or find one of the thousands already **meeting face-to-face**. More than 2,000 Meetup groups get together in local communities each day. You should be able to find groups specifically tailored to your target candidates' skills or interests.

With Naymz, your recruiters and marketers can calculate their influence across LinkedIn, Facebook, & Twitter; and compare their reputation against their peers and other Naymz members.

Weibo is the most popular social media site in China with around 250 million registered users and over 100 million daily visitors. A hybrid of Twitter and Facebook, messages are limited to 140 characters. Users have a verified identity (this is essential if you plan to use the tool) and can brand themselves by sharing content with images, music and video. If your company is expanding to China, find a way to network on Weibo.

 Viadeo is a Web 2.0 professional social network whose members include business owners, entrepreneurs and managers. Based out of France, the site had 65 million members by 2014. This is an excellent source for executive headhunting in France, Spain and Italy and can save you thousands of dollars in agency fees by getting your recruiters trained in how to use it.

 XING ("crossing") is a career-oriented social networking site enabling a "small-world" networking method for professionals. Based in Germany, it is used by people from over 200 countries. One unique feature I like about Xing is how it displays visually how each member is connected to any other member. I recommend it for sourcing talent in Germany, the Nordics, the Baltics and Russia.

Think about it now…

1. What social media platforms are appropriate for your job marketing and sourcing efforts?

2. Where are your top prospective candidates working right now?

3. Are you connected to any of these people on social media? If not, how and when will you get started?

4. What are you doing now to help with employer branding, marketing of your open roles or inviting top candidates to consider working for you?

STAR Hiring

Tap into YOUR network to bring in great candidates.

The first key to success in networking is for you and your team to have a **strong personal brand**. The following guidance applies to most social networking sites, but specifically is helpful for activity on LinkedIn. **These are just the basics..**

- **Complete your Profile**: Fully update your profile, including a picture, job history, overview of skills and contact information. Make sure you are linked to your company's profile page on each social media site where you have a page, and that you are using the most up-to-date logo/branding material provided by your marketing department.

- **Build your Contacts**: Synchronize your account with your email contacts from all available sources. Use the system tools to search for former colleagues, alumni of the schools you attended, and people affiliated with groups you might join. Review invitations you get from other people and accept all of those which are relevant to your career field.

- **Ask for and Give Recommendations:** Contact your previous co-workers, customers, managers (as appropriate) and subordinates and ask for recommendations. Reciprocate.

- **Join Groups:** Join groups and actively participate. Join groups that are relevant to your role and professional interests.

- **Answer Questions and Participate in Discussions:** Answering questions or participating in discussions should follow these basic rules: (1) **Relevant** to your career field; (2) **Polite**, humble and well-written; (3) **Helpful** to the person who started the discussion or asked the question.

- Post or link a **blog**, **white-paper** or **research project** to your Profile which shows off your area of expertise.

- **Post updates and share news about your job posting** on your social media accounts and in the groups which you have joined.

- Learn how to create **engaging and eye-catching posts about your requisitions**. Your recruiter should be creating posts as well, so you may be able to simply copy, share or re-post her updates.

Your Professional Network

TAKE SOME TIME NOW to write down the names of people you know, who might turn into prospects for either referrals or candidates for your future hiring needs.

PAST CO-WORKERS & EMPLOYEES	
NAME	CONTACT INFO

STAR Hiring

PAST BOSSES	
NAME	CONTACT INFO

MENTORS, LEADERS, INSPIRERS	
NAME	CONTACT INFO

FROM RECENT TRAINING - EDUCATION	
NAME	CONTACT INFO

STAR Hiring

PROFESSIONAL ASSOCIATION CONTACTS	
NAME	CONTACT INFO

CUSTOMERS / VENDORS / SUPPLIERS	
NAME	CONTACT INFO

Ask for referrals from your team!

Referrals from trusted colleagues make some of the best hires. They are generally more loyal, ramp up faster, and integrate better with your team.

Some cautions:

Some referrals are made because the source is trying to "help out" a friend. Make sure the candidate is rigorously screened for the skills and experience you need.

Some referred candidates have unrealistic expectations about the offer you can make them or the level of position they might attain at your company. Make sure you are clear with them, up front, about these expectations.

How do you solicit referrals?

> **Another Word of Caution**
> If you are contacted by an independent headhunter or agency recruiter, no matter how they phrase their "referral" of talent to you, they are 99.9% likely looking for a fee.

Think through the members of your team, colleagues in other departments, and trusted colleagues at partner companies, who should know great candidates for your role

Use the template messaging below to tap into your team and network to ask them for referrals.

Always guide your employees to use the official Employee Referral program (if you have one) so that they can qualify for a referral bonus payment.

STAR Hiring

Sample Request for Referral

Hello Team,

We are searching for a strong candidate for the role of [external title]. Please review the requirements below and consider referring a great-matching candidate.

We are looking for someone with the following skills and abilities (LIST 3 MOST IMPORTANT):
1. .
2. .
3. .

Submitting a referral at our company requires you to know the person and have their resume. Navigate to the intranet posting, click on the "Refer a Friend" button, follow the instructions to enter the candidate's information and upload their resume, click "Submit" and you are done!

Here is the intranet postings for the role: [link to your job posting on your intranet page]

Thanks team, for all you do!

YOUR SIGNATURE

Screening STARs

STAR candidates must be identified early and moved through your pipeline quickly. While we have discussed the necessity to attract, invite and provide a value proposition to these candidates, you also want to make sure you have a STAR in your hands to begin with.

Luckily for us all, STAR candidates are not shy about demonstrating their skill and discussing their past success. In fact, a STAR candidate often *expects* to be tested!

It is critical therefore, to give <u>all</u> of your candidates a thorough pre-screening before you move forward with costly onsite interviews.

What does this look like?

Assessing Technical Skills and Knowledge

You may find that only you and your team can adequately assess the technical skills needed by a candidate. You can also use various online tools, as we will discuss in a moment. But keep in mind the following:

- Requirements in the job description may be tested.
- Skills claimed in the Resume / CV may be tested.
- Verify that you are assessing skills actually employed in the job – nothing out of scope should be tested.
- Prepare your questions and who will ask them, in advance.
- Discuss appropriate answers and acceptable lines of problem-solving

STAR Hiring

Here is a Hack for FREE and effective testing of technical skills, by your own team: Use an instant-messaging tool and open a live chat box. Then pose a programming or design question in real time

Technical Skills Testing

You may choose to test technical skills prior to onsite interviews, and there are multiple resources to explore. **The key to a bullet-proof testing exercise is validation** of the test you are using to the skills required in your job posting.

Testing companies like **Prove It!, Brainbench** and **eSkill** tell you where candidates are strong and weak and how they compare to others who take tests covering popular technology.

CoderPad (https://coderpad.io) is a tool for conducting programming phone screen interviews. You can edit code and run it with your candidate, real-time in the browser. CodePad is another online interview tool & online code editor. CodeInterview is yet another and is currently available as a FREE Phone Interview tool.

While specific technical and theoretical questions (like "Give me the definition of…" or "What is the formula for…?") are necessary, they can get tiring. Also, they don't measure your candidates' problem-solving abilities. Likewise, brainteasers and trick questions often do not reveal candidate's skills. You may implement a problem-solving challenge, but make sure you validate the test, to the skills you intend to see employed by the candidate. More importantly, during the interview process, ask your candidates how they apply their theoretical knowledge on the job. Include situational and behavioral interview questions that show how candidates perform in real-life projects.

STAR Hiring

Here are some example technical questions for phone screens:

- Describe the troubleshooting process you follow for a program that keeps crashing.

- How can you debug a program while it's being used?

- Describe improvements you have made to your development environment (or IT infrastructure, or design flow).

- What's the most effective way you have used to gather user and system requirements?

- Describe a time you had to explain technical details to a non-technical audience.

- Where do you place most of your focus when reviewing somebody else's code? When and how have you applied this?

Resume Technical Scan

When scrutinizing examples from the candidate's resume, ask for clarifications, such as "Who were you working with?", "What was your role on the team?" and "What was the outcome of this project?"

STAR Hiring

The Phone Interview Process

Conducting a thorough technical and cultural review

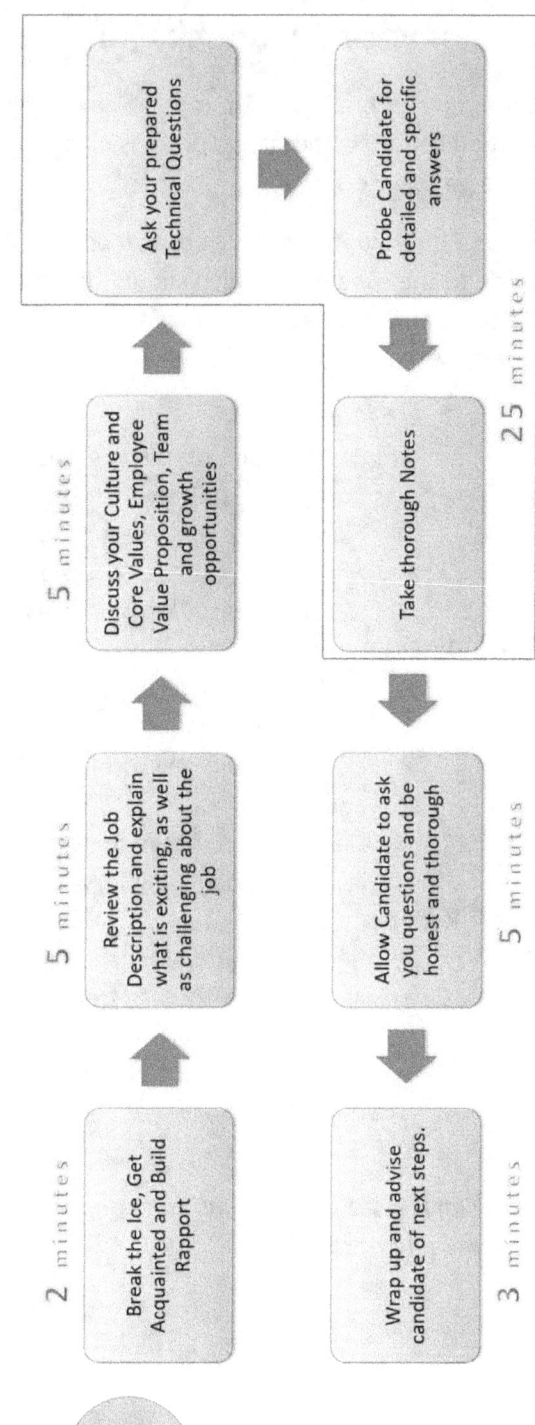

Send in your Feedback Quickly!

Your employer brand will improve by having better engagement with, communication to and timely processing of your candidates – and you will be happier too!

Here is a method for quickly getting feedback through to your recruiter, and on to the candidate, which should then help the hiring team decide on appropriate *next steps*, such as an onsite interview or declining to move forward with the candidate.

- Digest
    - Review your interview notes
    - Copy/Paste or Retype into Word Doc or Email
    - Clarify notes that are incomplete or illegible
    - Make sure that your notes are legally compliant! See the chapter on "keeping it legal" for guidance.
- Assess
    - Evaluate the appropriateness and quality of candidate responses
    - Use agreed-upon scoring methods and criteria consistently
    - Decide if you, based on this evaluation, would recommend moving forward.
- Report
    - Report to Hiring Manager and your recruiter
    - Make sure all notes / detailed feedback get to your recruiter
    - Decide and clearly communicate to your recruiter on next steps

Following is a set of forms you can adapt for your recruiters in their pre-screening of candidates...

Talent Screening, Part 1

Screener:	
Date:	
Candidate Name:	
Email:	-
Phone:	
Address or Location:	
Hiring Manager:	
Role(s)	
Current/Most Recent Employer:	
Highest degree completed:	
Years of directly related experience:	
Do you require documentation for legal employment?	
If YES, explain:	
Are you currently, or have you interviewed with us in the past?	
If YES, provide details:	
Are you open to other opportunities, in other Locations?	
If YES, explain:	
How did you hear about this job? If by Employee Referral, who?	
What's your current situation? Why are you looking?	
What are you looking for?	
Key Areas of Expertise and Directly Related Experience: (per the job description)	
Are you in the interview process with any other companies?	
Local?	
Relo Assistance Needed?	
How soon can you start?	

STAR Hiring

Talent Screening, Part 2

Screener:	
Date:	
Candidate Name:	
Email:	
Phone:	
Address:	
Hiring Manager:	
Role(s)	

Personality Assessment

Communication & Collaboration	
Energy & Passion	
Motivation & Perseverance	

Company Values Assessment

Rating Guidance:	0 = no positive indications of this value 1 = meets some of the positive indicators and can develop 2 = meets most of the positive indicators and "buys in" 3 = meets all of the positive indicators, role model

Value	Interview Notes	Rating (0 to 3
1		
2		
3		
4		
5		
OVERALL AVERAGE RATING:		

STAR Hiring

Talent Screening, Part 3

Screener:	
Date:	
Candidate Name:	
Email:	
Phone:	
Address:	
Hiring Manager:	
Role(s)	

Compensation

Current: Only document current compensation data if candidate voluntarily shares information

Current Base Salary	
Current RSUs or Stock:	
Current Annual Bonuses:	
Other Current compensation:	

Desired: Ask candidate for target or range. Data is needed to calibrate expectations, not to qualify or disqualify

Desired Base Salary:	
Desired Bonus Opportunity:	
Desired RSUs or Stock	
Other Desired compensation	
Job Level Desired (if specified):	

For an example of an interviewer assessment form to be used in a technical screening, look in the following chapter toward the end, for the Interviewer Assessment Form.

Chapter 7. STAR Interviewing

- ✓ Interview Planning
- ✓ Behavioral Interviewing
- ✓ Master Interviewer techniques
- ✓ Identifying motivation & persistence
- ✓ Realistic Job Previews

STAR Hiring

Interview Planning

Interview Format Guidance

The goal of interview planning is to have an efficient, comfortable (for all parties) and legal experience.

STRUCTURED INTERVIEWS

All of the research done on interviewing concur that a structured interview is the best method to insure consistent and accurate results. This is not to say that you do not adapt to the needs of the interviewers or candidate during the meetings, but that you are PREPARED with the questions you plan to ask, the correct range of answers to those questions and a previously designed system for selecting your top candidates.

- Well-defined job description / requirements
- Pre-determined interview questions
- Agreed-upon correct / viable answers
- Scoring, Ranking and Weighting of answers and of candidates
- Rules for eliminating or moving candidates forward
- Matrix for selecting top candidates

Guidance on how to plan these structured interviews follows.

PANEL INTERVIEWS

For efficiency and a robust assessment, and to protect you and our company, I also recommend panels of 2 – 3 employees, together, interviewing each candidate.

Panel interviews are conducted primarily during onsite interviews. They consist of a combination of 2 – 3 employees, together, interviewing each candidate.

A ratio of more than 4 employees to 1 candidate begins to feel intimidating for the candidate and should be avoided.

You can match interviewers on similar interests to gain efficiency. There should be less repeated questioning as they each need to know generally the same material.

You can also match interviewers on diverse interests to gain complexity. This inspires a more robust conversation and helps to fill in any potential gaps of silence, if interviewers can work well together.

Either way, a Panel Interview primarily helps you in that it provides legal protection from false claims of discrimination, by giving you witnesses for each interaction with the candidate.

STAR Hiring

Hiring Manager Interview Planning Form

Decide who will be on your interview team, what you want each person to focus on with candidates, and how they should evaluate candidate responses.

Interviewers and Focus Areas

Name(s)/Title (s)	Subject / Focus for Interview	Looking for what level of skill?

HM Interview Planning Checklist:

Questions:	Responses
Urgent?	
Travel OK?	
Video in place of F2F OK?	
Preferred interview room?	
HR to interview each candidate?	
Candidate to be tested on specific technical skills? (name them)	
Candidate to prepare a presentation? (if yes, describe)	
Candidate to present before a group? (if yes, who to include?)	

STAR Hiring

Get what you asked for!

Where do you start in choosing your interview questions? Should you look online for challenging puzzles and brain-teasers? Probably not. Should you ask your friends around the water cooler for their best challenging interview questions. Not until you have finished this training!

You should start building your technical and functional interview questions from the job description!

- Review the job description you published with your recruiter.
- Identify the measurable technical and functional skills required.
- Develop specific questions by which answering, the candidate will demonstrate proficiency in each of these skills.
    - See further information on how to develop BEHAVIORAL-BASED interview questions in later chapters.
    - Seek clear EXAMPLES of how the candidate has demonstrated each skill
    - Avoid hypothetical questions unless you are clearly testing a technical skill
- Ask your recruiter for online resources or ideas on questions if you need them.
- Determine ahead of time the measurement of "proficiency" you will require for each skill, for example:

Evaluation	Criteria	Score
Beginner	Somewhat skilled, able to learn and grow	1
Proficient	Consistent display of knowledge and skill	2
Exceptional	Exceptional/Outstanding, can teach others	3

- Determine the key indicators (what you want to hear or see from the candidate) to allow you to measure them across this scale.

STAR Hiring

Requirements Clarification Exercise:

1. Name a technical or professional skill you need to assess for a future hire

2. Name 3 key indicators which indicate mastery of this skill

    a. Knowledge of:

    b. Experience doing:

    c. Results that would indicate success:

3. How would the key indicators look if the candidate is...?

    a. Beginner

    b. Proficient

    c. Exceptional (STAR)

The Interview Process 45-minute to 1-hour plan

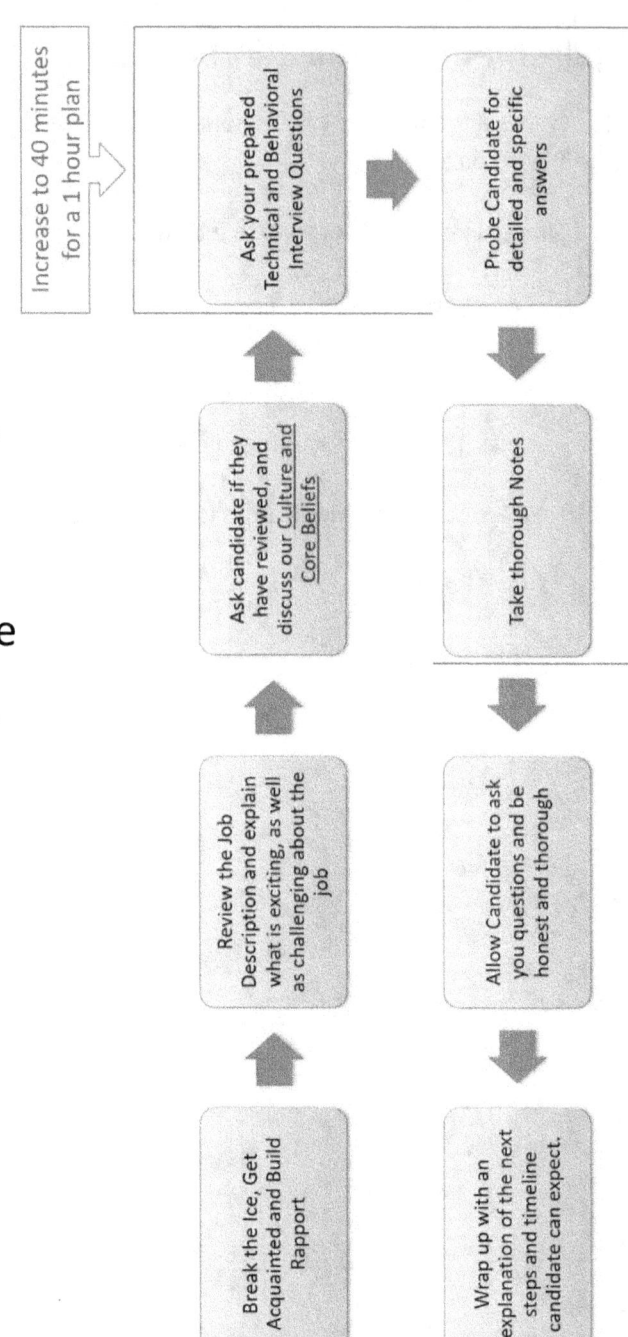

STAR Hiring

Assessing Technical Skills and Knowledge

- Anything required in **the job description** may be tested.
- Anything the candidate claims to know may be tested (usually on the resume)
- Prepare your questions and who will ask them, in advance.
- Discuss appropriate answers and acceptable lines of problem-solving with your team (ahead of time)

Written Tests should be validated by 3 or more qualified professionals and administered to EVERY candidate you interview onsite

White-boarding exercises may flow from an example from the candidate's resume, or a previously structured question

Presentations at the beginning of the day, in front of all onsite interviewers, can assess core technical knowledge and provide opportunities for many follow-up questions throughout the day

A Positive Candidate Experience

Your candidates become your brand ambassadors, for better or for worse. Candidates who connect with your company for job opportunities impact your external employer brand, by how they report to others about their candidate experience.

After applying to a job with your company, you can expect that most active candidates will immediately tell their friends and family, who will ask them repeatedly about how it is going. As they progress through the process, they will likely share details of their experience online, on social media and various rating sites, like Glassdoor or Yelp. Their sharing, whether it is positive or negative, can have an impact on sales of your products, trading of your stock, product branding and reputation, and motivation of your own employees. It will also definitely have an impact on your ability to attract, hire and retain STARs.

STARs want to know that they will be treated with respect, given a fair opportunity to compete, and be given consistent updates on the process and feedback from any interviews they have had.

Your recruiting or HR organization is hopefully working on efficiencies in its processes, such as status updates and interview coordination; and in providing a strong relational and consultative approach with candidates.

You (hiring manager) and your interview team will have a significant impact on the candidate experience as well. Here is how you can support a *positive* candidate experience.

STAR Hiring

Basic guidance for all interviewing situations

Tone of Voice:	Remain upbeat and positive. Even over the telephone, people can hear you smile.
Energy:	Keep a steady flow of energy, not hyperactive and definitely not a zombie.
Body Language:	Keep your body language open and engaged, arms at your sides or on the table, leaning forward slightly.
Handshake:	Firm and confident. Don't break their knuckles but make it memorable. Don't let go too fast but let go when they do.
Eye Contact:	Keep steady eye contact, but don't scare them. When your eyes move off to recall a story, re-engage soon. Make sure you make good eye contact with everyone in the room.
Remain in-doors:	If on the phone… Wind in the cell phone can ruin a good conversation and makes your candidate wonder if you are flying a kite or focusing on them.
Remain calm	…and generally still if on the phone. If you are moving around during the conversation, your shuffling and your breathing will be distracting.
Lay out your notes:	It is fine to refer to your notes or to take notes during a conversation, but you don't want to be flipping through pages as if you are lost. Lay your notes out in front of you… resume, questions, job description and a notepad.

Candidate Experience Assessment

In just a few, or one word, how would you generally describe the typical candidate experience at your company?

How easy is it to find your open jobs? How difficult is your application process?

How soon do candidates receive follow-up and status? How soon does the hiring manager, engage with candidates in the process?

What is your interaction like with candidates during pre-screening?

When candidates come in for interviews...

How are they greeted on arrival?

What is the environment like... meeting space, accommodations, etc.?

Are candidates given technical skills tests? Do they know this is going to happen? What does it look like?

What is the tone of questions from your interviewers? (soft and easy, engaged dialogue or an interrogation?)

When and how do you follow up with candidates after interviews?

When a candidate has had a bad interview, when and how do you let them know?

When a candidate has had a good interview, when and how do you let them know?

STAR Hiring

Hiring Managers

What you need to do: You're on a mission. You want a STAR and you want them soon. Focus is important. You need to:

1. **Select top talent for your team.** Be committed to the search for a STAR. Do not get side-tracked by internal company politics or pressure to hire someone you already know, just because it is easy and "safe." Remember, STARs will be competitive if you give them a chance.
2. **Know your business (technology, processes, future).** STARs will have questions about the future of your company and how they can learn, grow and progress in your company. Can you answer these questions?
3. **Partner with your Recruiter / Talent Acquisition Advisor.** Whether you are working with an internal recruiter or an agency, remember that this is a partnership. You need to have open communication about your needs, expectations, changes, pressures, and candidate engagements. Nothing should be hidden. If you cannot trust the recruiter you are working with, you should be looking for a new recruiter.

What you need to be:
1. **Absolutely sure of your needs.** Your needs may change before you fill a position, because of changes within your company, but you cannot enter into a STAR hiring process with a "wait and see" attitude. STARs will expect you to know what you want. So, while you may think you will know a great candidate when you see them, if you don't clearly communicate (and interview for) the areas of greatness (skills) you need, STARs will not come around nor will they stick around.
2. **Prepared... with a team of qualified screeners and interviewers.** The key word here is PREPARED. This whole workbook is focused on getting you prepared. You need to do your homework so that STARs are confident with you and your

team and impressed with your planning and process. Work with your HR or recruiters and develop a program that works for your organization.

Your interviewers should all have training on best practices and the legal do's and don'ts of interviewing. We do not recommend recruiting screeners and interviewers to your team just because they are a stakeholder. You can reserve those meetings for after your STAR is hired! Keep the team lean so you can move quickly through the process and stay focused. We also recommend that you consider who your back-up interviewers will be should you or another team member be absent. You do not want someone's absence to cause a delay of more than a few days.

Use the planning worksheet on previous pages to Consider now who you will recruit to your interview team.

3. **Have a strong sense of URGENCY.** Be ready to move fast on a STAR candidate. STARs will have multiple interview invitations, and even if you attract them while they are passive (not looking), you can bet that they will soon get another invitation after you have engaged with them. Generally, you should assume that a STAR candidate will have another offer within 2 weeks of you engaging with them.

STAR Hiring

Interviewers

What you need to do:

- **Welcome candidates.** Let candidates know that you are glad they are here, and not inconvenienced.
- **Ask open ended questions.** We will have more on this later as you learn Behavioral Interviewing skills and why this is a winning method for interviewing.
- **Listen and be patient.** As candidates answer your questions, make sure you are listening and that you are patient to allow them to answer you fully.
- **Connect with candidate.** Spend time with each candidate to get to know them, not just to interrogate them. You want to know if this is someone you will enjoy working with, and they want to know this also.

What you need to be:

- **You are the FRONT DOOR for your company.** Know your company's values, message and brand and speak well of it.
- **Focused on the Candidate.** The interview is about the candidate. Don't be self-centered and hog the time. If the candidate asks you lots of questions, answer quickly and turn the conversation back to them. This time is reserved to assess them, and you need to get it right!
- **Knowledgeable and skilled ...** (but not a know-it-all). Candidates are expecting interviewers to qualified in their role and qualified to assess them, but don't be a know-it-all or you will miss an opportunity to learn from a STAR candidate, and possibly miss the opportunity to clearly assess THEIR knowledge and skill.
- **Interested in the best interests of your company.** Sometimes the best decision is not to make a hire. Sometimes the best decision is to refer them to another team. Ask yourself, "is this a good, long-term employee? Should we share this candidate with another department?"

STAR Hiring

Interview Planning Discussion Questions

1. Are you open to using Panel Interviews? Why or why not?

2. How long do you want to plan each interview to last? Why?

3. What kinds of topics will you choose to "break the ice" with your candidate?

4. What do you need to do to be prepared to give a good introduction to the job for your candidate?

5. Will you use a skills test or technical test in your interviews? Who will develop this test or where will you get it? How will you validate the test and the answers? How will you score the results?

6. Are presentation and communication skills a strong requirement in your open position? Will you have your candidate give a presentation to a group as part of the interview? If yes, what should this look like?

7. Who will be on your interview team? (Go back and use the worksheet for this). Most important for you to think about now is whether they are adequately trained and of the right demeanor to be on your interview team... will they represent your company well, treat the candidates well and give you an honest assessment of each candidate? If not, what do you need to do to insure they meet these requirements before you begin interviewing?

STAR Hiring

Interview Confirmation

I have seen countless times when all of the interview planning and preparation is done internally, and the candidate is not communicated with about those plans, nor confirmed for the appointment(s) adequately or quickly enough... and then all of those plans fail.

One may assume that the recruiter should be in touch regularly with the candidate to keep them informed of the plans, but if someone else is making those plans, they may not have the information to share with the candidate. Likewise, if you have loaded your recruiter down with multiple requisitions or your open roles attract a high volume of candidates, the recruiter may not be able to keep up with all of the communication flow.

Regardless, some regular touch with the candidate should be maintained, about every 2 – 3 days, while planning is occurring, and a full and detailed interview confirmation should be sent to the candidate about 2 – 3 days before the onsite interviews, and at least 1 day prior to a phone interview.

The key ingredients of an effective interview confirmation include:

Date and Time: Include the arrival time needed to get into the facility and complete your check-in procedures.

Location: Provide the full address. Most candidates will copy that to their Maps app on their phone or GPS/Nav system. You can also provide a link to the Google Maps URL as well as driving directions, as an added touch. Make sure you are clear on where they can park and how to get through traffic to your site.

On Arrival: Describe the check-in procedures and any identification the candidate should provide. Indicate who will be greeting them on arrival and who will take them to their first meeting.

STAR Hiring

Agenda: Provide the details of their schedule of meetings for their visit, who they will meet with during each meeting, and generally what will be covered.

Interviewer information: As a best practice, especially for STAR candidates, I advise you to provide the full names, titles and URLs to online profiles of all interviewers.

Interview Follow-Up

Your recruiter should send an email soon after the completion of interviews to thank the candidate for their time.

STAR candidates will want to follow up with each interviewer to thank them for their time. This is the opportunity to go ahead and provide contact information to the candidate.

Lastly, make sure that you provide clear expectations on next steps, and a timeline to get feedback and results from the interview.

Most candidates will ask you for detailed feedback on their interview performance. Your legal team will ask you to refrain.

I advocate for communicating clearly and thoroughly with candidates, including the truth about where they fell short in an interview.

Refer to the chapters on Diversity and Legal Compliance for things you absolutely cannot reference and keep these communications strictly verbal.

Behavioral Interviewing

The premise behind behavioral interviewing is that the best predictor of future success, is past success in a similar situation. I do not dispute arguments around interviewing for a match to your culture and values, which is why we discussed that earlier in this book. Behavioral interviewing allows you to assess professional and technical skills, motivation, and values. It is a method of interviewing that elicits a story into which you can probe for all kinds of areas to evaluate your candidate.

Behavioral Interviewing is all about assessing things the candidate has actually done:
- successes and failures
- decisions and choices
- relationships
- learning

The keys to understanding why Behavioral Interviewing is successful is that:
- ✓ Behaviors are observable and verifiable
- ✓ Behaviors are fact
- ✓ Behaviors are not subjective
- ✓ Behaviors are not feelings or opinions
- ✓ Behaviors are not hypothetical

What does Behavioral Interviewing Sound Like?

In Behavioral Interviewing, you are asking candidates to tell you of actual examples of past efforts which relate to the job you are filling.

Ask Open-Ended questions. Open-ended questions are those which do not require a "yes" or "no" answer, a single result, date, or number. The question seeks a story.

Typically, you will **begin your questions** with openers like these:
- Tell me about a time when you…
- Give me a specific example of a project in which you…

As your candidate dives into their answer, you can then **probe** with:
- Tell me more about that example…
- I'd like to hear more about that project…

You can also probe candidates for specifics, as we will discuss further, which may require a "yes" or "no" answer, a single result, date, or number, but then you will want to encourage them to continue with, or wrap up their story, to make sure you have listened to them fully.

You will want to take notes while your candidate is talking, so make sure that you give visual and verbal cues that you are listening and want to hear more.

And finally, as your time will be limited, be prepared to interrupt when the story goes off track, or too long. You can even warn candidates ahead of time that you may need to do this, and make sure you do it politely, every time.

The Behavioral Interviewing Story

As previously stated, Candidate answers to Behavioral Interview questions should be in the form of a story. There should be a pattern to their answer. You can listen for these elements and take notes around each. If any parts of this story are missing, now you know what to probe for!

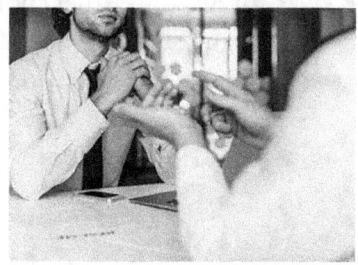

Listen for:

Situation: Which job on your resume are you talking about, where were you, what team were you on, what year was it, how many people did you work with and what was your role?

Trial: What was the key problem you needed to solve and what were the challenges in front of you? What made this particular experience MORE challenging than others you have experienced? (This element may be referred to as "Task" in other versions of the STAR story, but in my methodology, we focus on the "Trials" because these are what set STARs apart!)

Action: What did you do to address the problem, and specifically, what did you do to overcome the obstacles in your way?

Result: Did you win, meet your deadline, make the sale, build the product, or achieve your goals? What did these results produce for your company? This should probably have some kind of number… money and time are the most often results… i.e. "reduced production time from 2 weeks to 2 days." Or "saved $4M in outsourced vendor fees."

Let's Get Real ... Specific
Be wary of responses that contain little substance.
- Vague statements (fluff) or Opinions
- "What I always do in situations like that, is…"
- Theoretical or future-oriented statements
    - "would do,"" would like to do," "would have done"

Techniques to get specific / factual examples ... quickly
- During introductions and explanations of the interview process, tell candidate you will want to hear specific examples in their answers to your questions
- Lead the first few questions with "Tell me about a *specific* example of how you …"
- Ask candidate to recall the "most recent," "most interesting" or "most challenging" example.
- Describe the specific scenario you would like to hear about:
- "I would like to hear about a situation in which you accomplished X with a team of # or more, and the role you played on that team."

Behavioral Interviewing Exercise:
Write out 3 interview questions using the behavioral interviewing methodology. The first question should be around a technical or professional skill, the second around a key achievement and the third around team-fit or values. Then, pair up with a partner to practice asking these questions and probing for details in your partner's answers.

1.

2.

3.

What about going through the candidate's resume?

Yes, you still need to go through the candidate's resume. The most efficient way to do this is in parallel to your behavioral interview. As you are asking the candidate your pre-determined questions, ask the candidate to identify where in their resume you will find that example.

If the candidate has decided that a particular story is a highlight of their career, it should be in their resume. Can you find their stories in their resume? Do their answers to your behavioral questions line up to content in their resume? If not, why not?

Note that if you are interviewing a candidate for a new role they have not done before, or they are transitioning from a different field or type of role, it may happen that the story is not in their current resume.

In addition to tracking their stories to their resume, you will want to explore a few key areas in their resume to probe into their overall character and values.

Review their history:

- Why did they make moves? Did they leave jobs because they were progressing in their career, for more money, for better experience, or for a better work-life balance? Were they unhappy with the culture, their boss or their team? Why? Were they laid off or forced out due to a re-organization?

- Ask about short durations. You determine what a "short duration" is for your industry. In many, the minimum seems to be around 2 years, but in certain parts of the world, durations of 1 year are not unusual. Ask about these short durations and why the candidate could not have stayed longer.

Ask about their teams, managers and the culture of each organization. Whether they left any job for the culture, team or manager, it is also helpful to understand what they liked and didn't like about these elements at a few of their past jobs. Does your company culture or your management style align to the things the candidate is identifying as highlights of their career?

Techniques of Master Interviewers

Avoiding Interview Biases

Master Interviewers are masters of their emotions, body language and biases. This is not to say that they are stone-faced and unemotional. You will want to be natural, friendly and engaged, to give a great candidate experience. However, as discussed in the sections around Diversity, all people have some natural biases, or preferences. There are some interview biases you MUST try to avoid if you are going to become a Master Interviewer.

- **Stereotyping:** This is forming generalized opinions of a person based on his or her gender, background, appearance, etc. This is potentially illegal and always inappropriate

- **Inconsistency:** When you use different questions for different kinds of candidates, perhaps based on their gender or background, or even on their years of experience, you open yourself to legal liability and decrease your interview effectiveness across candidate pool. Metaphorically, you will be comparing apples to oranges.

- **First impression error.** This happens when you make a snap judgement (positively or negatively) based on the first few minutes of meeting a person. You might like their outfit, firmness of their handshake or their smile. You might dislike their haircut, that they do not stand up quickly, or that they shuffle some papers on the table. First impressions are sometimes correct, but when you are wrong – it is costly. Always re-test your assumptions. Did you not get a smile? Say something kind or funny and check again. Did you not get a firm handshake? Check again when they are leaving. And at the end of the day, do your preferences really matter for someone who needs to do the job you are trying to fill?

- *Halo effect.* This happens when something the candidate says or has done outshines anything negative you might hear, and you judge the candidate to be excellent without thorough examinations. A degree from the "right university" or one nearly "perfect" answer to a technical question is not the whole story for a candidate... keep probing and assessing and stick to your interview plan.

- *Horn effect.* This happens when something the candidate says or has done overshadows anything positive you might hear, and you judge the candidate to be unqualified without thorough examinations. Opposite from the Halo Effect, you are running the risk of passing up a great candidate if you don't give them a fair chance. Let this bias go and keep an open mind.

- *Similar to me error.* In this bias, a candidate who likes what you like and has a similar background to yours gets your preference. Similar to the Halo Effect, you may judge this candidate to be excellent without thorough examinations and miss a key flaw that will hurt your team or your company. And keep in mind that we don't need to clone you! Diversity is an asset to your company.

- *Candidate contrasting error.* In this bias, through the course of interviewing multiple candidates, one candidate stands out as "amazing" and all further candidates are judged inferior, even though they might be well-qualified. We are trying to hire STARs, and I want you to get that "amazing" candidate, but what happens if we can't hire the first STAR? Did you miss any other STARs in your assessment, because of this bias? Assess each candidate on their merits and rate them according to your predetermined scale. The best situation for you is when you have a VERY difficult choice between two or three GREAT candidates.

Overcoming Difficult Candidate Behavior

Really good interviewers have techniques to work around or push through all kinds of candidate challenges. Let's review a few of them here.

Candidate is ALL positive or ALL negative

What do you do when a candidate seems to say again and again, that he makes no mistakes, always gets the results desired, and simply can do anything he is asked? You seek contrary evidence. What this typically sounds like is this: "Tell me about a time when you did not get the results you wanted."

Candidate's answers sound REHEARSED

Have you ever heard a candidate give you what sound like "canned" or rehearsed answers? What did you do? The advice is to dig deeper and probe into the story or to ask for another example on the same topic – and to keep asking for new examples until you start hearing answers that don't sound rehearsed. Probing questions might include: "Why did you choose that option?"

Candidate answers with generalities

Behavioral interviewing is designed to elicit a story about a specific example, so what do you do when the candidate answers with generalities and hypothetical situations? That's right, you insist on specifics.
- Insist on specific details: Date, place, team, resources
- Insist on learning HOW they achieved their results

Candidate rambles and loses you

Because you are getting the candidate to tell you a story, there is a risk for some candidates that they will repeat themselves, provide too much background or explanation, or get off topic. The advice is to politely, but firmly interrupt and re-direct the candidate.
- Politely interrupt – do not delay!
- Re-state the question if it is still unanswered

STAR Hiring

Candidate is uncomfortably silent

Silence is tough to deal with for a lot of people. But if the candidate is uncomfortably silent, for 15 or 30 seconds, for example, this can get pretty awkward. You may have asked the candidate to think of their proudest achievement of all time. So you should give them enough time to think of their answer. If they simply cannot answer the question, you can move on to another question and possibly come back to this one later.

- Allow for at least 15 more seconds to hear an answer
- Politely re-phrase the question or move on to another (come back later)

Candidate is confused with line of questions

Lastly, if your candidate seems confused, and seems to be answering a different question than the one you asked, you may need to re-establish rapport, (break the ice again), then review the job description again, and start a few questions over again to re-boot the interview.

Interviewing for Motivation, Persistence and Perseverance

While integrating a Realistic Job Preview

- Motivation:
    - Motivation is the condition of being eager to act or work.
    - It is evident in an intense satisfaction with a behavior that drives one to do it repetitively.
    - **Motivation is strongly associated with passion**.
- Persistence:
    - Persistence, in simple terms is pressing forward, despite the obstacles, to finish what one has started
    - A persistent person is able to stay on task and maintain focus
    - **Persistence is strongly associated with self-discipline.**
- Perseverance:
    - Perseverance is not terribly different from persistence, but it involves more grit and more sacrifice.
    - Does the candidate muster their will to perform, even in the face of contrary impulses (failure, negative feedback, different results than expected)?
    - Does the candidate push-through and finish when faced with boredom, tedium, frustration, difficulty, and the temptation to do something easier and perhaps more pleasurable?

STAR Hiring

STAR Performers: (Review from Chapter 1)

3 commonalities in STAR Performers:

1. Confidence in Skill: I am GREAT at doing this
2. Can-Do Attitude: I CAN figure out a way to achieve this
3. Passion for Craft: I LOVE doing this.

How Achievement comes about:

4. Believe that you can do it
5. Overcome obstacles
6. Find solutions

2 consistent laws of achievement:

1. There are ALWAYS obstacles
2. Only those who find a way to overcome the obstacles get their goal

The "T" is for Trials

1. Just as a great novel or movie has a crisis, a great success story has a challenge. Characters with depth and stories with heart involve trials and challenges.
2. You got where you are by using your resources to overcome these trials.
3. You want to know how candidates overcome adversity.
4. A STAR candidate can identify these trials in their past and describe how they succeeded in the face of these barriers.

STAR Hiring

Motivation and Control...

- Locus of Control: is the extent to which individuals believe that they can control events that affect them.
- High performers have a strong Internal Locus of Control.

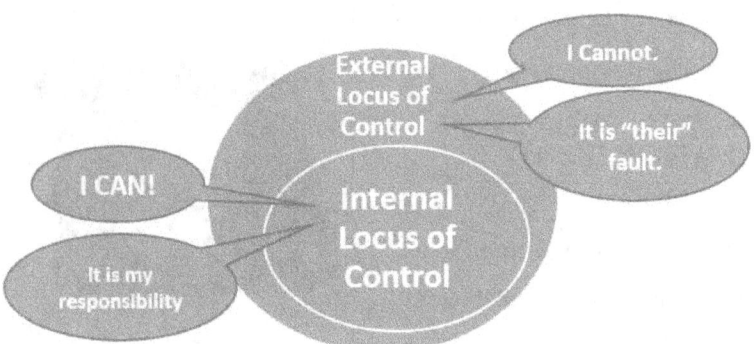

How Motivation-Based Interviewing works

1. Properly and consistently phrased skill and behavioral assessment questions using "How" questions.
   - "How have you been able to deal with time-pressure from your internal or external customers in the past?"
   - "How have you managed a situation where you needed to get results, but lacked all of the data or resources to get them?"
2. Ask for specific examples of obstacles they have overcome and listen to responses for predominant Internal ("I CAN") or External ("I CANNOT") locus of control.
3. Ask 3-5 questions about their passion.
   - What motivates you to come into work every day?
   - Who inspires you and why?
   - What's the greatest work day of your life?
   - Why did you choose this career-path?

STAR Hiring

Persistence and Perseverance
What am I listening for in the interview, to assess persistence and perseverance?
- Commits to action
- Shows personal courage
- Displays resilience
- Shows energy and drive
- Sustains high levels of effort following a setback
- Maintains momentum
- Maintains an optimistic outlook

What is a Realistic Job Preview (RJP)?

The RJP interview is structured in a way to increase transparency, reveal concrete expectations and provide insight into the cultural factors the new employee will encounter within the organization. Candidates consistently report desiring more specific, job-relevant information than they commonly receive

High turnover of new hires can occur when they are unpleasantly surprised by an aspect of their job, especially if that aspect is especially important to them.

A Realistic Job Preview consists of both positive and negative information regarding the position in order to give individuals a realistic view of employment with the company.

Critical components of an effective RJP include:
- Candor and openness
- Specificity about the job and its challenges
- A view of the work environment, preferably with employees actually performing common tasks and interacting
- Testimonials from current employees

RJP information should be focused on the things that matter most to the candidate and areas of the job or culture that correlate with engagement and turnover.

Design the RJP interview

Start by going beyond the job description and analyze a position with core questions to reveal deeper details, such as these:

1. How does this position contribute to the organization's overall success?
2. What unique contributions will the successful candidate make to the team?
3. What subtle challenges confront a person in this role?
4. What unique capabilities does the candidate need to succeed?.

> *The goal of questions like these is to spark a different kind of conversation, one that exposes the known complexities of the position and limits the remaining pockets of ambiguity to those unavoidable circumstances that can only be tested on the job*

Next, integrate your answers, through examples or stories, and weave them into your behavioral and skill-based questions

Uncovering Candidate Strengths

In <u>Soar with your Strengths</u> and <u>Strengths Finders</u>, I learned that uncovering strengths is a powerful process in the pursuit of excellence. Basically, strengths are the things you do well. Technically, a strength is a pattern of behavior, thoughts and feelings that produces a high degree of satisfaction and pride; generates a reward; and presents measurable progress toward excellence. There are five key characteristics of a strength, and you can uncover these through tactful interview questions.

<u>ONE: YEARNINGS:</u>
Characterized as the pull or attraction to one activity over another, a process that begins in early childhood.

Interview Question: What are the things you look forward to working on or that draw you back to work each day?

<u>TWO: SATISFACTIONS:</u>
Satisfactions are those experiences where the emotional and physical rewards are great. Competencies and satisfactions are not always partners. If it doesn't feel good, you are not practicing a strength.

Interview Question: Think of the things you do at work that consistently bring satisfaction.

<u>THREE: RAPID LEARNIG:</u>
If you catch on quickly to something you're likely to be good at it. Naturals are those who learn by "jumping in". Slow learning, however, is evidence of a non-strength.

Interview Question: What are some things you pick up very quickly at work? For example, within days, or even hours, others are asking you to show them how to do it.

FOUR: GLIMPSES OF EXCELENCE:

You can spot a strength by glimpsing a moment of excellence within a performance. One of the most effective ways to master this technique is by studying success.

Interview Question: Tell me about something you've done when you were complimented on your excellence, when someone used words like, "perfect, excellent job, or well-done."

FIVE: TOTAL PERFORMANCE OF EXCELLENCE:

Total performance of excellence is a flow of successful behavior, when there are no conscious steps in the mind of the performer. Total performance isn't a glimpse but the complete extension of an activity. It doesn't happen occasionally, but each time the activity is performed. One final test of total performance is the improvement of activity over a period of time. The satisfaction gained by total performance will cause a person to want to repeat it, but with repetition must come improvement.

Interview Question: Tell me about times when you have "lost yourself" in the execution of your work, when the effort was effortless, and the success was repeatable and sustainable.

STAR Hiring

Sample STAR Interview Questions

What questions can I ask to assess motivation, persistence and perseverance?

Following are sample questions you might integrate into your interviews which assess motivation, persistence and perseverance. Take notes on the questions you like, how you might modify them and when you might use them. Spot the elements of these questions which represent a "realistic job preview."

1. Tell us about the most challenging problem you faced last year that was difficult to resolve – one in which many solutions were tried, most failed, but you kept at it until it was solved.

    a. Probe with... How did you sustain your ability to keep going until you had fixed this problem?

2. You may face situations at our company when a project is going well and then it is hit by an unanticipated issue that puts it at risk, possibly even changing or cancelling the entire project. Urgent action may be needed, or you may be unclear about what to do next. People around you may become demotivated. Tell us about a similar situation you have faced and how you dealt with it.

    a. Probe with... If you could do it all over again, what would you do differently?

3. Major programs can take a long time to implement. You will need to find ways to keep momentum going and sustain your effort for the long haul. Tell us about a similar situation you have faced and how you dealt with it.

    a. Probe with... What did you learn from that experience?

4. Not everyone on your team or around the company will agree with your ideas – in fact, that's what we want to see! Tell us about a time when you initiated and pursued an idea in the face of opposition and criticism. How did you influence others to agree with you? What was the outcome? What would you have done differently?

5. In this job, you will face times of intense pressure... impossible deadlines, demanding customers (both internal and external) and extremely complex technical problems. Tell us about a time when you have faced this kind of pressure.

    a. What steps did you take to ensure that you were able to push forward?

    b. How did you respond to the pressure of this situation?

    c. What did you learn from that situation?

    d. What would you have done differently?

6. Everyone on this team with which you are interviewing has had to make decisions on the job about the delicate balance between personal and work objectives. Give an example of a time when you had difficulty balancing your personal and work objectives. What did you do? How did you deal with the pressure?

    a. Evaluating the candidate's answer: Did the candidate sacrifice time/plans/energy for the sake of a work objective, without compromising personal values or health? Was there resistance/low effort to make a personal sacrifice to reach a work objective? Was the candidate able to balance all objectives to his/her satisfaction?

STAR Hiring

7. Collaboration is central to the behaviors that make you successful at our company, but sometimes you have to work on something alone for a while. Tell us about a time when you were able to provide your own motivation to produce results even though you were working alone. What were the circumstances of the situation and how did you manage to motivate yourself?

    a. *Evaluating the candidate's answer:* Did the candidate have a performance strategy, which enhanced alertness, productivity, or efficiency? Was there compliance with a standard or requirement set by a team, manager, or organization?

8. Getting the job done may require unusual persistence or dedication to results, especially when faced with obstacles or distractions. Tell us about a time in which you were able to be very persistent in order to reach your goals. Be specific.

    a. *Evaluating the candidate's answer:* Did the candidate make an uncompromising commitment to a goal, as shown by long or flexible hours of work? Did the candidate find other creative ways to become more efficient, automate processes or recruit help? Did the candidate make appropriate choices to prioritize tasks and eliminate?

9. On this team, like most around our company, hard work is necessary in order to get results. You will face complex technical problems on the newest bleeding edge solutions. Tell us about a time when you had to work very hard to reach your goals and be specific about what you achieved.

    a. *Evaluating the candidate's answer:* Did the candidate make an unusual commitment in order to reach an objective, reflecting both high effort and accomplishment? Was there a routine response to work demands, rather than self-directed effort?

STAR Hiring

Interview Question Library

Accountability
1. What are your methods for keeping your supervisor advised of your status on projects?
2. Tell me about a time when you took responsibility for an error.
3. Tell me about a time when you were responsible for verifying the quality of a product or service before it went to the customer.
4. What have you done to further your own career development in the past 2 / 3 / 5 years?

Adaptability
1. Describe a major change that occurred in a job that you held. How did you adapt to this change?
2. What do you do when priorities change quickly? Give one example of when this happened.
3. Tell me about a time when you met resistance when implementing a new idea or policy. How did you deal with it? What happened?

Analytical Thinking & Problem Solving
1. Give a specific example of a time when you used good judgment and login in solving a problem.
2. Tell me about a time when you needed to develop and use a detailed procedure to successfully solve a problem.
3. Tell us about a time when you had to analyze information and make a recommendation.
4. Have you ever been caught unaware by a problem or obstacles that you had not foreseen? What happened?
5. Give some instances in which you anticipated problems and were able to influence a new direction.
6. There is typically more than one way to solve a problem. Give an example from your recent work experience that would illustrate this.

STAR Hiring

Attention to Detail
1. Describe a situation where you had the option to leave the details to others or you could take care of them yourself.
2. Do prefer to work with the "big picture" or the "details" of a situation? Give me an example of an experience that illustrates your preference.
3. Tell us me about a situation when it was important for you to pay attention to details. How did you handle it?

Courage
1. What is the most difficult decision you have ever made?
2. Describe a time when you faced impossible odds, but you knew you were on the right path?
3. Describe a time when you set aside your own needs for the good of another or the group.
4. Describe a time when you let go of your judgements or assumptions about people or viewpoints to work together on an effort.
5. Who would you identify as your top hero in life. Why? How have emulated this person?
6. Tell us about a major setback you have faced in life. How did you deal with it?
7. What has been your top work-related disappointment? What happened and what did you do?
8. What is the most competitive situation you have experienced? How did you handle it? What was the result?

Communication
1. Describe a situation when you were able to strengthen a relationship by communicating effectively. What made your communication effective? Describe a situation where you felt you had not communicated well. How did you correct the situation?
2. Describe the most significant written document you have ever completed.

3. Tell us about the most effective presentation you have made. What was the topic? What made it difficult? How did you handle it?
4. Tell me about a time when you presented complex technical information to a non-technical audience. What approach did you use and what was most challenging during that experience?
5. Describe a time when you were able to effectively communicate a difficult or unpleasant idea or result to a superior.

Conflict Resolution
1. When you disagree with your manager, what do you do? Give an example.
2. Give me an example of a situation where you had difficulties with a team member. What, if anything, did you do to resolve the difficulties?
3. Have you ever had to settle conflict between two people on the job? What was the situation and what did you do?

Customer and Colleague Relationships
1. Give a specific example of a time when you had to address an angry customer. What was the problem and what was the outcome? How would you asses your role in diffusing the situation?
2. Explain a time when you had to deliver bad news to a customer. What did you do to preserve the relationship?
3. What have you done to gain a customer's confidence? Give an example.
4. Tell us about a time when you built rapport quickly with someone under difficult conditions.
5. What, in your opinion, are the key ingredients in guiding and maintaining successful business relationships? Give examples of how you made these ingredients work for you.

STAR Hiring

Decision Making
1. How quickly do you make decisions? Give an example. Give an example of a time in which you had to be relatively quick in coming to a decision.
2. When you have to make a highly technical decision, how do you go about doing it?
3. Give an example of a time when there was a decision to be made and there were no procedures in place for the analysis or decision?
4. How do you involve your manager or other stakeholders when you make a decision?

Delegation
1. How do you make the decision to delegate work?
2. What work do you save for yourself, and what do you delegate to your team?
3. Tell me about a time when you had to recruit people who did not report to you, to take on parts of your work.
4. What was the biggest mistake you have had when delegating work? The biggest success?
1. What is the toughest group that you have had to get cooperation from? Describe how you handled it. What was the outcome?
2. Describe a project where you led a cross-functional team to meet tight customer deadline.

Diversity
1. Tell us about a time that you successfully adapted to a culturally different environment.
2. Describe a time when you made an effort to get to know someone from another culture.
3. Tell me about an experience as part of a cross-cultural team. What did you learn?
4. How have you helped to create an environment where differences are valued, encouraged and supported?

5. What measures have you taken to make someone feel comfortable in an environment that was obviously uncomfortable with his or her presence?

Influence
6. Describe a situation in which you were able to positively influence others in your organization to go in your desired direction.
7. Describe a time when you were able to convince a skeptical or resistant customer to utilize your services.
8. Tell us about a time when you had to convince someone in authority about your ideas. How did it work out?
9. Tell us about a time when you used facts and reason to persuade someone to accept your recommendation.
10. Tell us about a time when you used your leadership ability to gain support for what initially had strong opposition.
11. When you have difficulty persuading someone to your point of view, what do you do? Give an example.

Innovation
1. Describe a project or idea that was implemented primarily because of your efforts. What was your role? What was the outcome?
2. Describe a time when you made a suggestion to improve the work in your organization.
3. Describe the most creative work-related project which you have carried out.
4. Tell us about a problem that you solved in a unique or unusual way. What was the outcome? Were you satisfied with it?
5. When was the last time that you thought "outside of the box" and how did you do it?
6. Please give me an example of a project you were on that did not meet its goals. What were the root causes? How did you apply this learning to another project you worked on?

STAR Hiring

Integrity
1. Describe a time when you were asked to keep information confidential.
2. If you can, tell about a time when your trustworthiness was challenged. How did you react/respond?
3. Can you tell about a time when you chose to trust someone? What was the outcome?
4. Give me an example of a time you were supposed to follow a procedure but thought it may be incorrect. What did you do?
5. Tell me about a time when you had to report on your results, which were not positive or had missed your goals.
6. Give me an example of when you have found an error in your work and how you handled the situation.

Leadership & People Management
1. How do you coach an employee in completing a new assignment?
2. What have you done to improve the skills of your subordinates?
3. What was your biggest mistake in hiring someone? What happened? How did you deal with the situation? What was your biggest success in hiring someone? What did you do?
4. Tell us about a training program that you have developed or enhanced.
5. How do you evaluate the productivity/effectiveness of your subordinates?
6. How do you handle a subordinate whose work is not up to expectations? How do you deal with people whose work exceeds your expectations?
7. How do you get subordinates to work at their peak potential? Give an example.
8. Give an example of a time in which you felt you were able to build motivation in your co-workers or subordinates at work.

Negotiation
1. Describe the most challenging negotiation in which you have been involved. What were you negotiating? How did you prepare for it? How did you present your position? What were the results for you? What were the results for the other party?
2. Tell me about some areas which are non-negotiable when you are advocating for your company.

Organizational Skills Time Management & Project Management
1. How do you plan your day?
2. How do you decide what gets top priority when scheduling your time?
3. What do you do when your schedule is suddenly interrupted? Give an example.
4. Have you ever been overloaded with work? How do you keep track of work so that it gets done on time?
5. Describe a situation that required you to do a number of things at the same time. How did you handle it? What was the result?
6. Describe the most complex and detailed task you have had to complete in the last few months. How did you organize it? How did you get it done?
7. When given an important assignment, how do you approach it?
8. What have you done to improve your planning and organization skills?
9. Give me an example of a project that you took from start to finish while successfully meeting milestones and timelines.
10. Describe a project where you led a cross-functional team to meet tight customer deadline.
11. What do you see on average as the biggest hurdle in completing projects on time and how do you adjust to meet or exceed timelines.
12. Tell us about a time when you organized or planned an event that was very successful.

STAR Hiring

Risk Taking
1. Tell me about an experience working in a situation where the rules were not clear.
2. What is the riskiest decision you have made? What was the situation? What happened?
3. Give me an example of when you took a risk to achieve a goal. What was the outcome?
4. If you were tasked with starting your own business, what would you create? How would you start? Who would you involve?
5. Describe an assignment you have taken in your career that you knew very little or nothing about before accepting the role.

Self-Awareness / Emotional Intelligence
1. Recall a time when you were less than pleased with your performance.
2. In what ways are you trying to improve yourself?
3. What are your top 3 core values? What other values did you consider in choosing these? What have you done recently to publicly affirm one of these top core values?
4. What do you consider to be your professional strengths? Describe a specific example when you have used this attribute in the workplace.
5. What was the most useful criticism you ever received?
6. What is the most surprising way someone has described you?

Strategy
1. Some people consider themselves to be "big picture people" and others are "detail oriented". Which are you? Why?
2. How do you see your job relating to the overall goals of the organization?
3. Describe a time when you anticipated the future and made changes to current responsibilities/operations to meet future needs.
4. Tell me about the strategic plan in your most recent position. How was it developed? What was your role in developing that plan? How did you communicate it to the rest of your staff?

STAR Hiring

Stress Management
1. What kind of events cause you stress on the job?
2. How do you react when faced with constant time pressure? Give an example.
3. What was the most stressful situation you have faced? How did you deal with it?
4. When was the last time you were in a crisis? What was the situation? How did you react?

Teamwork
1. Some people work best as part of a group - others prefer the role of individual contributor. How would you describe yourself? Why?
2. What role have you typically played as a member of a team?
3. Describe a situation in which you had to arrive at a compromise. What was the end result?
4. Give an example of how you have been successful at empowering a group of people in accomplishing a task.
5. Tell us about the most effective contribution you have made as part of a task group or special project team.
6. Tell us about a time that you had to work on a team that did not get along. What happened? What role did you take? What was the result?
7. Describe a team experience you found rewarding.

Work Ethic
5. Tell us about a time when you had to go above and beyond the call of duty in order to get the job done.
6. There are times when we work without close supervision or support to get the job done. Tell us about a time when you found yourself in such a situation and how things turned out.
7. What projects have you started on your own recently? What prompted you to get started?
8. When you have a lot of work to do, how do you get it all done? Give an example.

STAR Hiring

Interviewer Assessment Form

Date:	
Candidate Name:	
Role:	
Interviewer:	
Focus Area:	

Rating Guidance:	1 = Needs Significant Improvement 2 = Needs improvement, is developing 3 = Consistent / High Performing 4 = Exceptional

Specific question / sub-topic	Notes	Rating

Overall Rating on this Focus Area	

STAR Hiring

Interview Exercise

Give an 8-Minute Interview

The 8-minute interview + 2-minute feedback... Total time for exercise = 30 minutes

Break into groups with 3 people per group:

1. Interviewer – Asking behavioral questions regarding motivation, persistence and perseverance.

2. Candidate – may choose to be "good" or "bad" with target behaviors, but mostly just be natural.

3. Observer – listen, observe and evaluate the interviewer – not the candidate

Conduct an 8 minute interview

Interviewer: Ask 2 or 3 questions from the examples given, or others your team constructs, weaving in a realistic job preview. Take notes and evaluate the candidate on a scale from 1 to 4, using the evaluation sheet included.

Receive 2 minutes of feedback from Observer

1. Asked appropriate questions?
2. Probed for specifics effectively?
3. Realistically portrayed the role?

Note that the Observer is evaluating the interviewer - not the candidate.

Rotate and Repeat

Until each person has done all 3 roles.

Chapter 8. Legal Compliance

- Overview of Legal Strategy
- Review your company policy
- Core areas to avoid
- Keeping good documentation
- Legal Quiz

Overview of Legal Strategy

Is it Legal?

Legal compliance, in its simplest definition is doing that which is permitted by law.

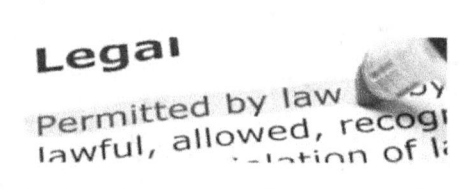

Sadly, in the employment and human resources world, compliance is much more complicated. One has to be wary of any behavior which would *appear* to be illegal or infringing on someone's rights. And more sadly, the lawsuits which arise from complaints of these behaviors can cost companies millions of dollars.

- August 2015, Target to pay $2.8 million for hiring discrimination. Some of the tests that Target once used to assess job applicants were big no-no's, according to the EEOC. (Fortune Magazine)
- November 2017, Con Edison paid $800K and revamped hiring and training practices after forcing disabled candidates to undergo medical exams and screening. (Reuters)
- March 2018, Google vigorously defended itself from a lawsuit against its YouTube subsidiary's hiring practice of excluding white and Asian men from its interview pools to fulfill its diversity goals. (Wall Street Journal)

Keep in mind that many businesses caused this very environment, by holding to practices which were discriminatory and intimidating. As a hiring manager today, you are also a gatekeeper and guardian for your company, protecting yourself and your company from horrible public relations and expensive lawsuits.

Most Lawsuits Result From poor communication, interviewer mishandling and candidate perceptions.

STAR Hiring

Legal and Regulatory Provisions

Key legal provisions in the United States which impact hiring:

The Civil Rights Act of 1964

Title VII of this act prohibits employment discrimination against members of protected classifications and makes it unlawful to limit, segregate, or classify employees in any way that would adversely affect their career progression. The protected classifications of this act were:

- Race, color and national origin
- Religion
- Gender

The act also prohibits discrimination because of pregnancy and prohibits sexual harassment. And the act also prohibits discriminatory pay practices.

Equal Employment Opportunity Act of 1972

This act expanded coverage for Title VII and established the Equal Employment Opportunity Commission, which continues to regulate, monitor and enforce these laws, including the administration of lawsuits against companies which are out of compliance.

The 1991 Civil Rights Act

This act added guidelines for punitive damages (how much you might pay in fines or if you lose a lawsuit). However, it also provided exceptions for work-related requirements, such as fitness requirements for firefighters; and Bona Fide Occupational Qualifications (BFOQs) for certain jobs, such as requiring a church pastor to follow the tenets of the faith of the church he or she might lead.

Age Discrimination in Employment Act of 1967

With revisions in 1978 and 1986, this act prohibits discrimination in employment for persons age 40 or older. It forbids a mandatory retirement age and it forbids limiting a protected individual from employment benefits, compensation or retirement plan assets because of their age. There is an exception for certain Executives if the company has other retirement provisions.

Rehabilitation Act of 1973

This act applies to federal government agencies and any federal contractor with contracts over $2,500. You would be surprised how many companies this may cover – yours may be one. This act prohibits discrimination based on physical or mental disabilities and requires employers to take affirmative action to hire qualified disabled people

Americans with Disabilities Act of 1990

Title 1 of the ADA prohibits discrimination against a qualified individual with a disability, because of the disability. A qualified individual is one who can perform the essential functions of the job with or without reasonable accommodation.

Reasonable Accommodation for a disabled person was defined as providing accessibility, re-designing work, and eliminating unnecessary qualifications, so long as these modifications do not cause an "undue hardship" to the business, usually in terms of cost. The business must prove this hardship if a complaint is filed by a qualified individual who believes he or she was not hired, purely because of their disability, when a reasonable accommodation could have been made.

Pregnancy Discrimination Act of 1978

This was an amendment to Title VII to clarify the prohibition of discrimination on the basis of pregnancy, childbirth or related conditions. It treats pregnancy as a medical condition and requires related benefits.

STAR Hiring

Vietnam-Era Veterans Readjustment Act of 1974

VEVRA applies to federal government agencies and federal contractors, and specifically protected Veterans with disabilities, and initially covered just those who served from 1964 – 1975. Many companies have committed to comply, and yours probably does also, by eliminating discrimination of any veteran who served in any conflict or war.

Immigration Reform and Control Act of 1986

This act prohibits discrimination against foreign-looking job applicants, but also establishes penalties for hiring illegal aliens. The IRCA does not allow preference for U.S. Citizens. Candidates must only verify that they are eligible to work in the United States for any employer, and employers must document this within 3 days of their start date using the Form I-9.

Employee Polygraph Protection Act of 1988

This act prohibits the use of lie detector tests in hiring and employment. Some exceptions are allowed for some security and pharmaceutical professions.

National Labor Relations Act of 1935

This act guaranteed workers the right to organize and join unions and labor affiliations and to bargain collectively. The act restricts companies from interfering with the organization of unions and it prohibits discrimination in terms of employment opportunities to persons who are members of unions. Later acts around unions allowed for workers to choose ***not*** to join a union ("right-to-work") and prevented employers from requiring membership ("closed shop").

Note that in none of these laws, is your company required to hire unqualified persons!

STAR Hiring

Review your company policy

Prohibiting discrimination and harassment in the workplace.

Most companies have a policy to afford equal opportunity for employment and promotion to all individuals regardless of race, color, national origin, religion, gender, age, marital status, veteran status, physical or mental disability. These are the primary classes protected under United States federal law, as previously explained.

Some companies also include sexual orientation, ancestry, citizenship status, medical conditions including genetic characteristics, a special recognition of pregnancy and childbirth, or any other basis protected by federal, state, or local law, ordinance, or regulation.

What does your company policy say?

Analyze your personal commitment *You demonstrate your company's values when you publicly affirm and act on each value, with and among your colleagues; and when on your own.*

Have you publicly affirmed this policy? When and how?

Have you spoken to your team about adhering to the policy? If not, when and how will you do this?

Have you taken action to correct any situation you may have seen that might violate the policy? When and how?

What training do you need, and what does your team need, to be 100% in compliance, and even champions of this cause?

STAR Hiring

Play it Safe!

During your screening, interviews and follow-up with candidates, for thorough legal compliance and security, it is best to never discuss...

Age:
Birth date, Graduation dates, ages of children

Race, color or national origin

Avoid questions about where they were born or their accent, for example.

Religion
Avoid questions about religious preferences or practices, required holidays, etc.

Gender or sexual orientation
No relevance to whether person is qualified for the job - continue assessment of qualifications.

Citizenship or visa status
Should be handled through recruiter pre-screening, but generally, can only ask if they are eligible to work in the country for any employer.

Arrests, bankruptcy and credit
Handled through your background check process

Disability
Do not inquire about visible conditions. Candidate may share that they have a disability and need an accommodation. Defer discussion to HR and continue assessment of qualifications.

Language skills
Only ask if it is a requirement of the job, and then you should test every candidate equally.

STAR Hiring

Height and weight

Never directly ask someone's height or weight. Potential appearance of discrimination around medical conditions, gender, ethnicity.

Marital status / Pregnancy

Avoid questions about name changes /spouse /children (plans to have children or get pregnant)

Unions or political affiliations

Avoid asking about Union memberships. Best to avoid most political affiliations also. Potential violation of national labor laws.

Documentation

Legal experts agree that you need to document your notes and experiences in your interviews...

WHY?

- **Assures consistency:** You can show evidence that you followed the same process for each candidate – a best practice for legal compliance.

- **Makes record of events:** To protect you and your company from false claims of discrimination or harassment, you and your colleagues have a written record of the events. This is even more effective if two or more interviewers have worked together as a "panel interview" team as previously recommended.

- **Permits review of record prior to decisions:** you can quickly access your documentation to move forward with status to candidates and offers to your target hires!

- **Helps defend management actions:** As you move forward in your internal approval process, your documentation supports the offer you want for the candidate and any exceptions needed to get your STAR aboard!

WHO?

- **All interviewers** should document their interview notes. Consider using the Interview Evaluation forms presented earlier in this program.

- The **Hiring Manager** should gather all notes from all interviewers, review them for accuracy and compliance, then turn them over to **HR** or your recruiter (preferably at the "Selection Meeting" ... see further materials on this) for safe-keeping.

STAR Hiring

WHEN?
- Recall is a tricky thing. The best advice is to take notes during the interview and tidy them up immediately after event, sending them on to the next phase.

WHAT?
- It is important to document facts - NOT opinions or conclusions. For example, you might write, "Candidate claimed to have expertise in Lean & Six-Sigma, but could not name each step in DMAIC." However, you would not write, "Candidate was grasping for straws when challenged on Lean & Six Sigma knowledge."
- An exception to this rule is when you are tasked with assessing a candidate's personality, culture-fit or core values. On the last of these it is easy to say, "Candidate claimed to have a strong core value of trust and loyalty." But you may also need to state, "Candidate demonstrated executive presence with confidence and composure," which is clearly a judgement-call.

RULES OF THUMB
- Avoid physical descriptions to remember candidates
- Focus on qualities of promising candidates, vs. those you do not intend to pursue
- Don't include information that cannot be the basis for an employment decision
- Don't include ambiguous references

STAR Hiring

Legal Compliance Test

Circle whether the question is safe or not safe to ask when interviewing a candidate.

What is that accent I hear? Where is it from?	Safe	Not Safe
What have you researched and learned about our company?	Safe	Not Safe
It's not on your resume, so in what year did you finish your bachelor's degree?	Safe	Not Safe
What are your hobbies?	Safe	Not Safe
Are you pregnant or planning a family?	Safe	Not Safe
Can you work overtime?	Safe	Not Safe
Tell me about your proudest achievement last year.	Safe	Not Safe
Do you have a disability or any past medical problems?	Safe	Not Safe
Have you ever been fired? Why? What did you learn from it?	Safe	Not Safe
How many children do you have?	Safe	Not Safe
Are you involved in any professional organizations or networking groups?	Safe	Not Safe
Are you a citizen of this country?	Safe	Not Safe
Why do you want to work at our company?	Safe	Not Safe
Do you go to Church on Sundays?	Safe	Not Safe

Legal Compliance — Answer Key

Is the question safe or not safe to ask an interviewing candidate?

What is that accent I hear? Where is it from? *Not even if you are from the same place!*	Safe	**Not Safe**
What have you researched and learned about our company? *Great question for every interview!*	**Safe**	Not Safe
It's not on your resume, so in what year did you finish your Bachelor's degree? *There is a reason it is not on their resume!*	Safe	**Not Safe**
What are your hobbies? *Can lead to interesting insights, but can also get you off-topic – be more precise.*	**Safe**	Not Safe
Are you pregnant or planning a family? *Never safe!*	Safe	**Not Safe**
Can you work overtime? *No problem, if the job requires overtime, but you might want to explain it.*	**Safe**	Not Safe
Tell me about your proudest achievement last year. *Great question for every interview!*	**Safe**	Not Safe
Do you have a disability or any past medical problems? *What do you do when the candidate brings up a disability... when you observe a disability that is NOT mentioned by the candidate?*	Safe	**Not Safe**
Have you ever been fired? Why? What did you learn from it? *OK to ask – good insights from this question.*	**Safe**	Not Safe

STAR Hiring

How many children do you have? *Candidate might mention their kids and might ask you about yours – how should you deal with this?*	Safe	**(Not Safe)**
Are you involved in any professional organizations or networking groups? …… *What would make this question Not Safe?*	**(Safe)**	Not Safe
Are you a citizen of this country? *What information is really needed and how should it be acquired?*	Safe	**(Not Safe)**
Why do you want to work at our company? *Good question, but a little "blunt." How could you ask it more tactfully?*	**(Safe)**	Not Safe
Do you go to Church on Sundays? *What can you ask about Sundays?* *What do you do when the candidate mentions days or times they cannot work?* *What do you do when the candidate brings up their faith?*	Safe	**(Not Safe)**

Chapter 9. Selection Best Practices

- The Selection Meeting
- Planning and Preparation
- Evaluation Tools
- Running the Meeting – Getting a Hire!

The Selection Meeting

It's Decision time!

After your formal onsite interviews with your top candidates, it should be standard practice to schedule a Selection
Meeting. These meetings are sometimes referred to as "Interview Debriefing" or "Feedback Roundtable" meetings. I use the term "Selection Meeting" to set the tone correctly. You are coming in to this meeting to select the best from among the best – and to MAKE A HIRE!

Who should be involved?

All key members of the interview team should be invited. You may have involved some people in the interviews who would be peers or subordinates to the selected new hire, for the sake of socializing, acquainting and making the candidate comfortable. The "key" interviewers are those whom you tasked with assessing specific selection criteria.

You should also think to invite your Recruiter / Talent Acquisition Advisor and possibly someone from the HR Team, especially if they were involved in early candidate identification or screening, or during your interviews.

When should the meeting be held?

Best practice would be that this meeting is scheduled automatically by your talent acquisition operations support person or your executive admin team, when they are arranging the finalist interviews.

Another best practice to consider is to book all interviews with your top shortlist of 2 – 3 candidates within the same week or two, and host one Selection Meeting so that you can compare and contrast your finalists and make a complete and fully-informed decision. Regardless, hiring managers should provide instructions for how they wish these Selection Meetings to be arranged, in their onsite interview scheduling requests.

STAR Hiring

How do I plan and prepare?

Gather your Team: Advise all Selection Meeting participants that you need their involvement. Work with your recruiter or admin to schedule an appropriate date for the meeting.

Review the Job Requirements: Review the Job Description you advertised for the role. What did your team agree are the positive indicators for success in each of the job criteria? Can you quantify these?

Develop your Evaluation Tool: Use the sample tools at the end of this chapter or ask your recruiter for other ideas. Or develop your own tool *to fairly evaluate* all candidates against the stated job requirements

How do you facilitate and manage the Selection Meeting?

I believe you have two key options on how to manage your selection meeting. In option 1, you lead the meeting and stay neutral and objective. In option 2, you ask your recruiter or HR to lead so that you can participate more fully in the discussion. The steps for running an effective meeting are simple, if you have prepared…

1. Open with a review of the job description and requirements
2. Review what each interviewer was assigned to analyze
3. Go through the review – use the tools!

The Goal is to Get a Hire!

Lead with the idea that you are here to **make a hire!** Remind team that STAR candidates were selected and that each of them met or exceeded the requirements of the role to get into the interview. Use your evaluation tool or the whiteboard to get a visual representation of the ranking and comparisons of your top candidates. Require each person to give thorough, factual input. Allow for debate, but don't allow the discussion to derail the decision. *Ultimately, you (the hiring manager) have the final decision.*

The 5 C's

Are you ready to make an offer? It is natural to pause at this time and reflect on the person you have identified. You may only get to hire a few people in your organization this quarter or this year. Even if you are hiring many people this year, you know that every one of them can help your company win or lose. You want to be SURE.

There are five basic areas where you must make a match, to move forward to an offer.

1. **Competency:** Has the candidate sufficiently demonstrated that he or she has all of the required (and most of the preferred) knowledge, skills and abilities? Go back to your job description and make sure you are getting each requirement checked off that list.

2. **Chemistry:** Often considered to be the most important consideration, the candidate's chemistry with the team, and the people in your organization can make or break a good hiring decision. Do they relate well with their potential new co-workers? Did conversations naturally to drift into common interests and values? Did you find yourself and the candidate smiling and laughing some, when appropriate? Did you and your team genuinely enjoy their company?

3. **Character:** Do the candidate's values match the values of the organization? Did he or she research the company's stated values and did he or she express a shared interest in those values? During your interviews, did you ask detailed questions about your company's core values? Are you confident that the candidate understands your company's values and adequately communicated how hers or his values make a match?

4. **Culture:** Each organization builds a unique culture, made up of the various traditions within the organization. Is it a very energetic organization focused on branding and product identification? Do you stay late and burn the candle at both ends, or is it a more balanced commitment? Are you environmentally conscious? Do you value community service? Does your team have some regular lunch or happy hour traditions? During the course of your interviews, did the candidate fit well with these traditions?

5. **Compensation:** Does the candidate's target compensation range intersect with yours? Can you assemble a total compensation package that meets his or her needs and fits within your budget? Do you need to stretch that budget? Can you? How comfortable are you with this? This is not just a "gut check." Ask your recruiter and your compensation team to analyze the data. Consider internal equity, market data and more. Refer to the chapter on offering and negotiating for more guidance on this subject.

STAR Hiring

Selection Tool Sample

Date:	
Hiring Manager:	
Role / Requisition:	

Rating Guidance:	1 = Needs Significant Improvement 2 = Needs improvement, is developing 3 = Consistent / High Performing 4 = Exceptional

Candidates	Hiring Manager:	Recruiter or HR:	Interviewer 1 Name:	Interviewer 2 Name:	Interviewer 3 Name:
	Focus Area:	Focus Area:	Focus Area:	Focus Area:	Focus Area:
	Highlight & Rating:	Highlight & Rating:	Highlight & Rating:	Highlight & Rating:	Highlight & Rating:
1.					
2.					
3.					
4.					
5.					

STAR Hiring

Chapter 10. Negotiating, Offering and Onboarding STARs

- ✓ Compensation
- ✓ Making a Good Offer
- ✓ Delivering the Offer
- ✓ Offer Approval
- ✓ Offer Letters
- ✓ Preventing Counter-Offer Loss
- ✓ Offer Acceptance
- ✓ Onboarding

Compensation

I have found that everyone, from recruiters to hiring managers to candidates fear and resist the compensation conversation. All too often, this becomes a barrier in either the candidate consideration, or offering phase. I train my staff to open the conversation early and dive deeper into the details at every touchpoint with their candidates.

Aligned with some recognizable phases of the recruitment process, here are some suggestions on how to open, develop and refine the compensation conversation.

Job Requisition Phase:

A compensation study should be run against market data **and** internal equity should be assessed to accurately define your agreed salary range for the role.

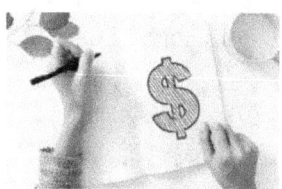

Determine the Job Level / Grade, Incentive Eligibility (if any), and secure approval from your Compensation Manager

Budget and ranges should be agreed so that the Recruiter can discuss either generally or specifically and negotiate with top selected candidates.

Screening & Interviewing Phase:

Recruiters, PLEASE acquire precise information on the candidate's current compensation and benefits. Discuss candidate expectations for future compensation. Answers such as "I am just looking for a competitive offer" and "I will need an increase" must be clarified and defined.

Assess whether your candidate should be pursued further based on the data you obtain.

After candidate interviews onsite or via video/teleconference with key decision-makers, sees the company and understands the job, clarify all of the compensation data again... current and expected.

Follow-up Phase:

While interviews are ongoing with other candidates, continue to communicate with top candidates. Ask top candidates about other opportunities they are pursuing and projected compensation with those other opportunities.

When near time to make offer, open a conversation about the offer you expect to extend ("float the offer") to get candidate feedback.

Pre-negotiate salary (with no obligation on either side) and discuss details such as benefits, perks, hours.

Offer Phase:

HR (and in best cases, the Recruiter) should be authorized to make the offer within a pre-determined range – with no additional approvals necessary.

Extend the offer with the best terms possible according to pre-negotiating discussions. You may, if you believe the candidate has a "negotiating-mandate" by their cultural background or personality, leave room in the offer to add a little more salary or benefits.

Do not be offended by a candidate who wishes to negotiate. Be authentic and as much as possible, be transparent about what authority you have to improve the offer, and how much negotiating your company will do.

Be VERY clear when you are at the point of delivering your FINAL offer. Close the candidate and secure a start date as soon as possible.

STAR Hiring

Compensation Analysis Worksheet

The Approved Range

Job Title			
Location			
Grade			
Bonus Target			
Salary Range	Min	Mid	Max
RSU Range	Min	Mid	Max
Sign-on:			

Comparisons

Comparable Employees	Title	Salary
1		
2		
3		

Candidate's Current Salary or Competitive Offer

	Current
Est. Base	
Est. Bonus	
Stock or other	
Retention Bonus	

Annual Target Cash	$ -

Recommended Offer

Base Salary	
Bonus	
Stock or other	
Sign-on	
Total Annual Target Cash	
Increase or Loss ()	
Comp-a-ratio	

STAR Hiring

Offer Work-Out

Propose an offer for a <u>STAR Candidate</u> for this role with the understanding that she interviewed very well and appears to be as gifted as your highest paid comparable employee.

Job Title	Senior Software Engineer		
Location	Austin, TX		
Grade	5		
Bonus Target	15%		
Salary Range	$90,000	$110,000	$140,000
RSU Range	$10,000	$30,000	$50,000
Sign-on Bonus (up to:)	10%		

Comparable Employees	Title	Salary
1	Sr. Application Engineer	$95,000
2	Senior Software Engineer	$105,000
3	Senior Software Engineer	$120,000

	Current		Recommended Offer?
Est. Base	$100,000	Base Salary	
Est. Bonus	15%	Bonus	
Est. Stock or Incentive	$20,000	Stock /Cash	
Retention Bonus		Sign-on	
Other		Other	
Total Annual Target Cash	$ 135,000		$
		Increase or Loss ( )	
		Comp-a-ratio	

STAR Hiring

Making a "Good Offer"

In a competitive marketplace, you should make the best and most fair offer you can make for the talent you wish to acquire.

Gather data from the external market and salary surveys from industry-leading firms and compare that data to your internal equity to develop recommended salary ranges, stock awards, bonus levels and other offer details.

Internal equity should be based on all current employees in similar roles and grades, not just your own team. If comparable members of your team are significantly below the recommended salary for a role, work should be done with HR to correct this, but it should not keep you from hiring great external talent.

Knowing what is a "good offer" for your candidate begins early in the recruiting process and your recruiter should be allowed to have in-depth conversations with your candidates about their current and expected compensation.

Early discussion (at least before onsite interviews) with your recruiter of appropriate offers with your top 2 – 3 candidates is strongly advised.

Delivering the Offer

Your recruiter, Talent Acquisition Advisor or HR Manager should always deliver verbal and final offers.

These professionals should be trained in negotiation skills and knowledgeable in market demands, competitive offers, company benefits and other information needed to complete the transaction. Review the earlier chapter around Negotiation Skills you should expect your recruiters to know.

Help your Recruiter/HR help you by equipping them with any competitive intelligence you may have obtained in your conversations with candidates. Have they shared their "real" target salary or percentage of increase they desire with you? Do you know what their peers are making?

Sometimes it is necessary to make an initial offer below the numbers you expect to close at with the candidate, because the candidate demonstrates a propensity for negotiating terms during the course of interviews. Your Recruiter/HR should be aware and anticipate this, but if you have noted it yourself, make sure that you advise your Recruiter/HR of this information.

Offer Approval

Your Recruiter/HR will have preliminary and pre-closing conversations with your target candidate(s) to insure that they sign the final offer you give them. This is often referred to as the "Verbal Offer."

STAR candidates know that no offer is final until it is put in writing. Your company likely has a formal Offer Approval process to document what you have committed to your target candidate. Make sure that all notes and justifications for these approvals are saved together.

If any changes are required because the candidate has requested more compensation, or if you offer a package below his or her clearly stated expectations, the approval process will likely have to be repeated, so make sure you get it right the first time!

STAR Hiring

Offer Approval form

Candidate Name	
Requisition #	
Business Unit	
Location	
Job Title	
HRIS Job Code	
Job Level / Grade	
EEO Job Class	
Full-Time or Temp	
Target Start Date	
If Temp / End Date	
Hourly or Annual	
Base Salary / Pay Rate	
Annual Bonus Target	
RSUs / Stock / Equity	
Retention Bonus	
Sign-On Bonus	
Relocation Allowance	
Car Allowance	
Housing Allowance	
Wellness Allowance	
Approval Routing (Electronic Signature preferred)	
Hiring Manager	
HM+1	
Finance Approver	
HR Approver	
Executive Approver	
Recruiter (issue offer letter)	

Offer Letter

What is an offer letter?

After your recruiter pre-closes your STAR candidate on the terms of the offer, and you complete your formal offer approval process, it's time to send an <u>offer letter</u>. Typically sent before you run a background or reference check, but before signing an official employment contract (if you need one), this letter formally offers a position to a job applicant, summarizes the main terms and conditions of the offer, and provides details about the role and company to help a candidate decide whether to accept the offer.

The offer letter should NOT be the starting point for employment negotiations. As we have said, your recruiter should have conducted extensive conversations with the candidate about required compensation and benefits, and pre-closed the candidate around the terms you will extend in the offer letter. The offer letter should be a *confirmation* of the already-accepted terms and conditions.

If the candidate accepts your offer, they should sign the letter and return it to you. However, it's important to understand that an offer letter is not always a legally binding employment agreement. This is typically a separate document that provides detailed legal protection for both parties.

What is included in an offer letter?

An offer letter provides a brief overview of the position and company and includes specific job details, like start date, salary, work schedule, and benefits. There is no legally required format for a job offer letter. You may use, delete or reorder the elements described below to fit your company and the roles you're filling.

Company Logo
To convey professionalism and authenticity, use your company's official letterhead with a high-resolution image of your company logo.

Date and contact information
Include the date, the candidate's first and last name (full legal name), and their address. If a specific party or entity in your company is responsible for the sending and receiving of the offer letter, you might also want to include their contact information as the sending party – however – your company letterhead may sufficiently cover this.

STAR Hiring

Greeting / opening paragraph
Start your offer letter by addressing the potential employee using "Dear," followed by their first and last name. *It is best to use the candidate's full legal name.* Congratulate them and express enthusiasm in offering them the job with a positive, upbeat opening line, like: "We are excited to offer you a position at [Company Name]!" You can make this opening line as formal or casual as you like, depending on your company's culture.

Job details
Begin your letter with specifics about the position, as well as work logistics. This should include the formal title of the position, the anticipated start date, full- or part-time status, the office location, their manager/supervisor, and a brief description of the role and its responsibilities. This gives the candidate an idea of what to expect and helps clarify any details that may have been misunderstood or overlooked during the interview process.

Compensation
Use the offer letter to clearly explain the compensation package. Include specific details about how much the candidate will be making on an annual or hourly basis, how often they will get paid, and the available payment methods. You should also provide detail on equity (stock/RSUs/options), bonuses, commission structures, etc., as applicable to the role or the person.

Also, if the offer includes any allowances (car, housing, meals, wellness, memberships, travel, training/conferences, etc.), detail them here. The compensation section may cover multiple paragraphs. This is not a problem – the focus is to cover everything necessary to convey the whole package.

Benefits
To encourage a candidate to accept the job offer, summarize the key benefits your company offers. If you plan to hire STARs, it is better to provide some information here about your benefits, than to just say that they will be informed during orientation of what you have for them. However, you might also attach a benefits summary / overview to your offer letter and simply reference that attachment here.

STAR Hiring

Either way, you should not need to provide too many details, since your day-one / orientation program should go into detail and offer new hires the time to consider their options and enroll in your programs. In the offer letter, you might briefly mention attractive benefits, such as:

- Insurance coverage
- 401(k) plan
- Paid time off
- Flexible spending accounts
- Educational assistance
- Flexible work hours
- Work from home options

Contingencies
If the job offer is contingent upon the candidate completing certain documents or performing certain tasks, mention this in the letter. These contingencies might include a background check, drug test, signed confidentiality agreement, waiver to future patents and intellectual property, clearance for export control licenses for protected technology or intellectual property, reference checks, or I-9 form / proof of employment eligibility in the country where they will be working.

At-will status
To prevent creating contractual obligations, include an at-will statement. This is primarily a clause for the United States, but other countries allow it too. Every state (except Montana) is an at-will state, meaning that both the company and its employees can terminate employment at any time for any reason. For help determining what language you should use when describing an employee's at-will status, it's best to seek legal guidance to avoid any unintended consequences. Some sample language is provided below.

Disclaimer
To reduce any confusion, consider including a brief disclaimer to explain that the letter is informational and not a legally binding contract or agreement. Consult a lawyer to avoid including contractual implications.

STAR Hiring

Expiration date
Remember to provide an expiration date on the offer. STAR candidates typically respond well to a timeline of around 72 hours to accept or decline your offer (up to 5 calendar days for high-level STEM jobs), and less favorably to a 24-hour deadline. You will find however, that many candidates – including STARs – will sign your offer immediately, if you have given them an exceptional candidate experience and the offer fulfills all of the terms you previously negotiated. A hard deadline will also prevent you from losing other qualified candidates (other STARs, hopefully) if your #1 STAR declines your offer.

Closing
End your offer letter by expressing excitement about welcoming the candidate to the team! This is referred to as an "assumptive close," meaning that you are assuming the candidate will accept and sign your offer. If you have done a good job with the candidate experience and offered exactly what you promised in your negotiations, you should assume this! Inserting an assumptive closing here gets the candidate into the same mindset. Provide contact information in case they have questions about the offer details. Include instructions on how the candidate should sign and return the offer letter and include a line for the candidate to sign and date the offer if they choose to accept it. You may also want to provide a line for the candidate to enter their anticipated start date, to either confirm the date you previously listed, or to enter a new date if circumstances have changed.

STAR Hiring

Job offer letter template

[Company Logo]

MM/DD/YYYY

Candidate First and Last Name
Candidate Address
City, State, Zip

Dear [Candidate Name],

We are pleased to offer you the [full-time, part-time, etc.] position of [job title] at [company name] with a start date of [start date], contingent upon [background check, I-9 form, etc.]. You will be reporting directly to [manager/supervisor name] at [workplace location]. We believe your skills and experience are an excellent match for our company.

In this role, you will be required to [briefly mention relevant job duties and responsibilities]. *(OPTIONAL)*

The annual starting salary for this position is $[dollar amount] to be paid on a [monthly, semi-monthly, weekly, etc.] basis by [direct deposit, check, etc.], starting on [first pay period].

In addition to this starting salary, we're offering you [discuss stock options, bonuses, commission structures, etc.].

Your employment with [company name] will be on an at-will basis, which means you and the company are free to terminate the employment relationship at any time for any reason. This letter is not a contract or guarantee of employment for a definite amount of time.

As an employee of [company name], you are also eligible for our benefits program, which includes [medical insurance, 401(k), vacation time, etc.], and other benefits which will be described in more detail in the [employee handbook, orientation package, etc.].

We are excited to have you join our team! If you have any questions, please feel free to reach out at any time.

STAR Hiring

Sincerely,

[Your Signature]

[Your Printed Name]
[Your Job Title]

Please confirm your acceptance of this offer by signing and returning this letter by [offer expiration date].

Signature: _____

Printed Name: _____

Date: _____

STAR Hiring

Background Checks, References and Verifications

Generally, all the below activities should take place after you have given the STAR candidate their offer letter. Checking references may occur before the offer letter is given, as a contingency, but you should communicate this to your STAR candidate in advance.

Reference Checks

Reference checking is a good process for confirming what you have seen during your interviews and hopefully for learning some new information to reinforce your decision to hire. Rarely will you uncover negative information in a reference check, because the candidate has likely picked the people who will say the best things about them.

Some employers will contact people who were not provided as references by the candidate, if they know that these people have worked with a candidate before. If this is done without the candidate's knowledge, it is called "back door references." I do not recommend this. First, you may harm your future relationship with the candidate by infusing distrust, and second, you could set yourself up for a legal challenge of discrimination.

If you do wish to contact other people who are not provided as a reference by the candidate, simply ask the candidate!

Communicate how you know the person and why you wish to reach out to them. A STAR candidate should have nothing to fear and will often agree, and then your actions are honest and open.

Following is a template format you can use via email to request reference names and contact information from the candidate, and then I provide a format to follow up with those contacts to obtain the reference information.

STAR Hiring

REQUEST REFERENCE INFO FROM CANDIDATE

Subject: Request for References for [Candidate Full Name]

Hi --,

I am pleased to report to you that your interviews have gone very well, and we need to move forward to request your references. We try to keep this very simple, by emailing to each person with the same brief questionnaire. Please provide the following names and email addresses:

- 2 managers
- 2 peer co-workers
- 2 internal or external customers

Thank you!
YOUR SIGNATURE

REQUEST REFERENCE INFO FROM REFERENCES

Subject: References for [Candidate Full Name]

Hello [Reference First Name],

I am very happy to let you know that we have had successful interviews with [Candidate Full Name] for a role at [Your Company Name] and we are discussing a potential offer. Your colleague has provided your contact information as a person who can provide a professional reference. We are interested in hiring new team members who will continue to help us [insert your mission statement]. I would like to make this process easy for you by asking you to respond by email to the following questions:

STAR Hiring

Your name, current job title and employer:

1. What is/was your professional relationship with, and how many years have you known [Candidate Full Name]?

2. What would you identify as the top strengths of [Candidate Full Name]?

3. What would you identify as areas for professional growth for [Candidate Full Name]?

4. Please rate [Candidate Full Name], using a scale from 0 to 4 on the following items, and add any comments to each area you feel are necessary:
    a. Technical Skill & Learning Ability

    b. Innovation & Creativity

    c. Collaboration & Communication

    d. Accountability & Perseverance

5. Are there any other comments, content, praises or concerns you would like to provide us?

Thank you again for providing this reference! If we at [Your Company Name] can be of any further support to you in your own career pursuits, please let us know.

YOUR SIGNATURE

STAR Hiring

Background Screening

Background screening is done to verify that you are hiring a person of good character, who will remain honest and perform consistently in your organization. Legal experts suggest background checks to protect the company from liability. Should a future employee cause damage, and they had a negative criminal or credit history you could have known about, you could be liable for those damages.

You will need to outsource this service to a highly reputable company with a strong history and proficiency in checking backgrounds. The two companies I have used most in my career are HireRight and ISP/Promesa.

The 3 main pieces of information you will want to verify are:

1. Identification. Using the social security number, previous addresses and other identifying information provided by the candidate, your background check company should verify that these data match with the person you have interviewed and want to hire. This process takes a matter of minutes and is done entirely online.

2. Criminal History. Using the identification information, your background check company will verify the candidate's arrest and conviction history by the cities, counties, states and countries where they have previously lived. The timing of this process varies depending on the number of locations where your candidate has previously lived (as an adult) and how remote or rural any of those locations may be. It is typically all done online, again, depending on the locations being checked.

3. Credit History. This data is only checked if the person you are hiring has a fiduciary responsibility in your company. That means that they have a responsibility for managing money for your company, and they have access to that money. It typically applies to staff in Accounting, Finance and Payroll areas.

A number of municipalities, States in the USA, and countries around the world, are beginning to restrict companies from checking criminal or credit history. In some cases, the restrictions are around the method and timing of the checks, and in other cases, the restrictions are around what can be checked. Understand and follow the laws in each location for your company.

Education, Certification and License Verification

Education is the one area of a background check that has the most potential for holding up the process and delaying the start date of your new hire. Educational institutions are not the most efficient when it comes to providing quick and easy access to student data. You will need to decide if this verification is really necessary. If the skills one would obtain from the education are what is absolutely required, and not necessarily the degree or diploma, then verify that the candidate has the skills! However, if your company has a policy of granting titles, such as "Engineer" only to those who have obtained a degree that purports to certify one for that title, then you will want to verify the attainment of that degree. One easy hack at this process is to ***communicate early*** with candidates that your company needs to verify their degree for them to have the title they want, and that you will need them to provide a copy of their transcript or diploma. Most background check vendors will collect this for you and authenticate the documents.

Professional licenses and certifications are typically easier to obtain, because the entities that provide them are in the business of verifying this information for employment. You may still need to ask the candidate to obtain the documentation, but often your vendor can log into a database to retrieve the necessary verification

STAR Hiring

Employment Verification

You probably want to verify past employment because the candidate will have leveraged their past work experience as their qualification for joining your company. This is another area that can cause delays however, due to the way this data is verified. That is, the candidate will not remember exact dates of joining and leaving certain companies in their history, but your vendor will attempt to verify the service according to precise dates. Additionally, previous employers contacted to confirm employment history may be unresponsive.

You will want to ensure that your vendor has a robust online system with a team of qualified agents who will follow up on this. At the end of the day, you will also want to provide flexibility to approve a background check that is still incomplete due to an unresponsive past employer.

Work Authorization

U.S. employers must check to make sure all employees, regardless of citizenship or national origin, are allowed to work in the United States. This is done by completing the Employment Eligibility Verification (I-9) Form, and reviewing documents showing the employee's identity and employment authorization. You may also use E-Verify, which I strongly recommend, and you may be required to use the E-Verify system in certain states

Federal law prohibits employers from conducting the Form I-9 and E-Verify processes before the employee has accepted an offer of employment, nor can you require someone perceived as "foreign" to produce specific documents, such as Permanent Resident ("green") cards or Employment Authorization Documents.

STAR Hiring

Applicants may be informed of these requirements in the pre-employment setting by adding the following statement on the employment application:

> "In compliance with federal law, all persons hired will be required to verify identity and eligibility to work in the United States and to complete the required employment eligibility verification form upon hire."

Recruiters may ask if the candidate is eligible to work in the United States, but they should never specifically ask if the candidate is a United States Citizen, nor generally "how" they are eligible.

Recruiters cannot require a candidate to provide documentation to support their claim or work eligibility, until an offer of employment is made.

That said, STAR candidates who do require documentation for work eligibility are sensitive to the needs of the company to verify their work eligibility. They will often provide detailed information on how they are eligible or what documentation they will require, if the recruiter simply asks,

"Are you eligible to work in the United States for any employer or will you need support from our company to obtain documentation?"

Preventing Counter-Offer Loss

STARs will get counter-offers and other offers from your competitors. You and your team need to be prepared, and you should address this EARLY.

By early, I mean during the recruitment process, as soon as you begin interviewing the STAR candidate. Your recruiter or you, will ask the STAR candidate if they are interviewing with other companies, or internally with their current employer.

As you build your relationship with the STAR candidate, and discover more about them and their job search, you should then begin to address the possibility of other companies making them an offer. Your recruiter should be trained in how to do this.

The most effective prevention or protection against a counter offer by a current employer or a competitor is a GREAT OFFER for a GREAT JOB with a GREAT MANAGER, working on a GREAT TEAM.

Standard Treatments of Counter Offers (before they are made)

Current Employer:

- **Ready to Go:** You've decided to make this move, so can you decide now NOT to entertain a counter offer from your current company?

- **Too Little – Too Late:** If they could have offered you something better before, they should have, right?

- **Foot out the door:** If you stay there, you are the person who has announced you are ready to leave, so it is best to cut ties.

STAR Hiring

Other Companies:

- **No Bidding Wars:** We don't want to get into a bidding war – let's decide now what a Great offer looks like and get that for you. If I do that, will you accept it without entertaining any other offers?

- **Beat their Pending Offer:** Learn about the details of other pending offers and beat them

- **Uncover Competitor's Weaknesses:** Research the current market information about companies competing for your STAR and find their weaknesses... but make sure your company has overcome those same weaknesses! As necessary, discuss this research with your candidate.

Onboarding

Remember that your new hire is not locked in until they show up for Day 1.

Job searching candidates consider **the whole candidate experience** as part of your recruitment program. You should also. Even though certain steps and processes are handed off from recruiters, to administrators, to HR, and back to the hiring manager, the process should be seamless, efficient, well-communicated and overall, a premium experience. <u>STARs will have this expectation.</u> All too often, the Onboarding Process is a place where companies fail their STARs.

This training program and workbook are not designed to cover in detail, the whole onboarding process. Much more can be said about the people, processes and tools required for a premium experience. In fact, it could be as much as an entire new day of training, and a completely new workbook! However, let me try to give you an overview of the key components needed to onboard a STAR, and to...

Get Your STAR Hire Set Up for Success!

<u>Over-Communicate!</u>

Your new hires are hungry for information. Who is my primary contact as we move through onboarding? How will my background check be processed and how long will it take? What documentation is still needed, when do you need it, and what purpose does it serve? What will my first day look like?

Some companies try to cover all of this with one big email. Others put it all on a website and send the candidates a link. I recommend that you answer these questions, in the order you see them above, one-by-one, with a personal and direct communication (email or phone call), allowing the candidate to reply directly back to a person with any additional questions they might have.

As you keep feeding this information to candidates, also continue to send them updates on what is going on at the company, with their team, or with the products or services they may be supporting in their new role. This can (and should) be managed by the hiring manager and his/her team. This approach gives the candidate a sense of belonging well before their first day, helps them to visualize themselves even further, in their new role, and builds loyalty with the company.

Provide automation

While the communication needs to be personal and direct, the systems need to be seamless and automated. If you want to hire STARs, who will bring you a 250% return on investment against "bad hires," then invest in the right software to handle applicant tracking and offer approvals, electronic signature collection, data transmission to vendors for things like background checks, reminders, updates on company activity, and onboarding portals where candidates can upload required documentation.

Equip managers with tools and guidance

Best practice calls for companies to set up a hiring manager onboarding portal, where all of their questions can be answered about the onboarding process and their responsibility, and they can find links to systems and tools. If your company is still building on this, at least set up a FAQ page with basic information and directions. Bottom-line for hiring managers is, stay engaged through the onboarding process, work with your HR or Admin team to keep things moving, and stay in touch with your STAR!

STAR Hiring

Be Ready for Day 1

As soon as you have confirmation on the accepted offer, hiring manager, get busy ordering equipment, tools, uniforms, computers, software, phones and other supplies so that your STAR has a GREAT Day 1. Think of your own experiences on Day 1 at some of your past employers. I am sure you have some crazy stories about the chaos you experienced. The worst experience is when you start a job and you are "dead in the water." You have no tools, so you cannot work – you feel useless and lost. If you have hired a STAR, and probably invested more company resources for that new hire, then you want them productive as quickly as possible.

The other major thing to consider for Day 1 is communicating with your team. Who needs to know about this person coming aboard? Will she have a trainer, a mentor, a small team she needs to meet? Get them lined up! Let them know what your STAR is like, what she needs, what she knows, and what you expect from them as they help you get her onboarded.

Make Day 1 EPIC

Too often I see companies really downplay Day 1. They run through some paperwork, walk them around the building, and drop them off at their manager's desk. Then the manager, who is swamped with busy-ness, parks them at an empty desk to twiddle their thumbs while he finds someone to "babysit" them until he can schedule a couple of hours of 1:1 time – which might be tomorrow.

> Things epic are those of heroic proportions which far surpass the ordinary, especially in size, scale, and intensity.

STAR Hiring

A STAR day-1 experience should include:

- Manager and team greet them on arrival, with smiles, welcome gifts, a company shirt or coffee mug, introductions, and a written agenda for the week, including a scheduled lunch with the team on Day 1. (imagine if your company has 10 new starters from 10 different teams... that will be an amazing party in your lobby!)

- HR take them to orientation where there is breakfast, coffee, comfortable chairs, windows and space to breath.

- Spend time with new hires letting them get to know each other. Have them say why they joined the company and talk about their hiring experience. Consider inserting a fun activity or ice-breaker here.

- Orientation includes a personal visit from a local executive with a welcome to the company, followed by video introductions from other executives who could not be there in person. Next, they should see a video on the company culture and values, current performance and goals, and outlook. Wrap up the morning with an overview of the company structure and how it operates, and personalize it with a focus on the specific business units or departments represented in the new hire class. Consider building a game or activity where new hires "run the company."

- Hand off to Hiring Manager and team for that team lunch.

- Orientation continues with required paperwork and must-do training or policy review. Save the heavy training around sexual harassment or discrimination for a later meeting, or an online course, but make sure your company values are clear – which should preclude these behaviors, among others. Remember that this is the afternoon, right after lunch, so break up the training with some games, activities and snacks.

STAR Hiring

- Orientation wraps around 3 - 4pm. Escort new hires to hiring manager, or have managers come get them, to take them to their team area.

- At their desk or work area, awaits a decorated space with welcome signs, notes, streamers, etc. The work area is fully equipped and functional, allowing the new hire to immediately log on or power-up and test things out.

- Greeting the candidate are his trainer for Day 2, his mentor for his first few months or year, and other team members nearby.

STAR Hiring

Plan Week 1 and Beyond

Having seen what an Epic Day 1 looks like, you, Hiring Manager, can see that you have a few things to prepare...
- a welcome lunch
- trainer and mentor
- equipment
- welcome gifts and decorations

You may not be gifted with this kind of planning or social arrangements. No problem! Recruit members of your team to help. Get everyone involved.

Here are some other things to plan for Week 1 and beyond:

- Plan a happy hour for the end of week 1. You, your STAR and your team will deserve it!

- Line up reading materials, research, technical training.

- Schedule critical 1x1 and group meetings.

- Schedule any immediate travel that must occur.

- Register or make reservations for your STAR to attend conferences, customer meetings, offsite trainings, etc. which may occur within 3 weeks of Day 1.

- Develop 30-60-90-day goals and a tracker (spreadsheet or other tool) so that you and your STAR can be confident that things are moving as planned.

About the Author

Dan Medlin

Austin, TX
dan.medlin.starhr@gmail.com
http://www.linkedin.com/in/danmedlin
http://danmedlin.wordpress.com/
https://www.facebook.com/AustinStarHR

Dan Medlin is a senior Talent Acquisition leader with over 20 years of experience building return on investment in people. He has expertise in strategy, branding, sourcing, candidate experience, hiring manager training, recruiting and training teams; and delivering peak headcount. He also consults companies around employee performance, engagement, culture and rewards. Dan has worked in companies ranging from 75 to 275,000 employees, including GE, Samsung and AMD.

Dan published the **STAR Career Workbook** on Amazon.com, a cost-effective alternative for job seekers in career transition, and this book, **STAR Hiring**, as a result of a successful round of professional training sessions and consultation projects with business clients to help them navigate and WIN the talent war.

Dan founded and leads StarHR, an executive recruiting and talent acquisition consulting firm based in Austin, TX. StarHR specializes in bringing in great talent for High Tech companies, locally and globally. For any questions or needs on the services of StarHR, contact Dan at dan.medlin.starhr@gmail.com.

Dan Medlin firmly believes in the grace of Jesus Christ to save and lead everyone who puts their faith in Him to an abundant life. It is by His grace and the prompting of the Holy Spirit that this book was written.

Dan lives with his wife and children just south of Austin, TX. They are partners with Vertical Chapel, a thriving Christian church. Dan serves on the Board and plays bass guitar on the Worship team. Dan's wife, Lisa leads an adoption and foster care ministry called Embrace. Dan & Lisa have 5 children (two adopted), from ages 5 to 23.